SCHOLASTIC

Teaching With Favorite
READ-ALOUDS
—in First Grade—

**50 Must-Have Books With Lessons and Activities
That Build Skills in Vocabulary, Comprehension,
and More**

By Susan Lunsford

p9. 29 - weekend w/wendall

New York • Toronto • London • Auckland • Sydney
Mexico City • New Delhi • Hong Kong • Buenos Aires

Teaching
Resources

DEDICATION

For Brad, Ryan & Madison:
Here's to a lifetime of sharing great books together.

To Colleen and Marge and their first graders:
Thank you for all your hard work and your smiles, too.

To Joanna and Sarah:
Thanks for your guidance and support.

Cover design by Josuè Castilleja
Cover photography: Reid Horn/Corbis
Interior design by LDL Designs, based on a design by Sarah Morrow
Interior illustrations by Sharon Holm

ISBN 0-439-40418-5

Printed in the U.S.A.

5 6 7 8 9 10   40   10 09 08

CONTENTS

Introduction: Formula for First-Grade Success 5

CHAPTER 1: WELCOME BACK TO SCHOOL!
10 Must-Have Books to Kick Off the School Year 7

   Mini-Lesson in Action: *Emily's First 100 Days of School* by Rosemary Wells . . . 8

   Miss Malarkey Doesn't Live in Room 10 by Judy Finchler 13

   Yoko by Rosemary Wells 14

   Chrysanthemum by Kevin Henkes 15

   Arthur's Teacher Trouble by Marc Brown 16

   Best Friends by Steven Kellogg 17

   Leo the Late Bloomer by Robert Kraus 18

   David Goes to School by David Shannon 19

   Never Spit on Your Shoes by Denys Cazet 20

   Thank You, Mr. Falker by Patricia Polacco 21

CHAPTER 2: LET'S CELEBRATE!
10 Must-Have Books for Rainy Days, Birthdays, and Other Special Days . . . 23

   Mini-Lesson in Action: *Thunder Cake* by Patricia Polacco 24

   Jimmy's Boa and the Big Splash Birthday Bash by Trinka Hakes Noble 28

   A Weekend with Wendell by Kevin Henkes 29

   Arthur's Birthday by Marc Brown 30

   The Art Lesson by Tomie dePaola 31

   Owl Moon by Jane Yolen 32

   Night Tree by Eve Bunting 33

   Alexander and the Terrible, Horrible, No Good, Very Bad Day by Judith Viorst 34

   The Polar Express by Chris Van Allsburg 36

   Song and Dance Man by Karen Ackerman 37

Reproducibles 38

CHAPTER 3: ROCKING AND ROLLING WITH WORDS
10 Must-Have Books with a Beat 42

   Mini-Lesson in Action: *17 Kings and 42 Elephants* by Margaret Mahy 44

   Noisy Nora by Rosemary Wells 48

   Feathers for Lunch by Lois Ehlert 49

   Zin! Zin! Zin! A Violin by Lloyd Moss 50

   Miss Spider's Tea Party by David Kirk 51

   A Hippopotamusn't by J. Patrick Lewis 52

Something BIG Has Been Here by Jack Prelutsky 53
Where the Sidewalk Ends by Shel Silverstein 54
Good Books, Good Times! by Lee Bennett Hopkins 55
There Was an Old Lady Who Swallowed a Fly by Simms Taback 56
Reproducibles 58

CHAPTER 4: HOW MUCH? HOW LONG? HOW MANY?

10 Must-Have Books for Teaching Math and Science **60**

   Mini-Lesson in Action: *Knots on a Counting Rope* by Bill Martin Jr.
     and John Archambault 61
   How Much Is a Million? by David M. Schwartz 64
   Seven Blind Mice by Ed Young 65
   A Chair for My Mother by Vera B. Williams 66
   The Bookshop Dog by Cynthia Rylant 67
   The Grouchy Ladybug by Eric Carle 69
   Tops and Bottoms by Janet Stevens 70
   Frog and Toad Are Friends by Arnold Lobel 71
   Stellaluna by Janell Cannon 72
   Miss Rumphius by Barbara Cooney 73
Reproducibles 74

CHAPTER 5: PURPLE COATS, PURPLE PURSES, TYPING COWS, AND TALKING DOGS

10 Must-Have Books for Teaching Reading and Writing **76**

   Mini-Lesson in Action: *The Relatives Came* by Cynthia Rylant 77
   Frederick by Leo Lionni 82
   Dr. DeSoto by William Steig 83
   Martha Speaks by Susan Meddaugh 83
   Author: A True Story by Helen Lester 85
   Frog, Where Are You? by Mercer Mayer 87
   Click Clack Moo by Doreen Cronin 88
   The Purple Coat by Amy Hest 89
   When I Was Young in the Mountains by Cynthia Rylant 91
   Lilly's Purple Plastic Purse by Kevin Henkes 92
Reproducibles 93

50 Must-Have Books for First Grade **95**

Grade 1 Learning Skills **96**

Formula for First-Grade Success:

Build a Book-Based Classroom Beginning with 50 Must-Have Books

There's no better way to settle a group of rambunctious six-year olds than to sit down in front of them with a great book. Elbows nudge and loud *shhhhs* can be heard as those who are unaware quickly and quietly gather for the read-aloud. For the next twenty minutes, readers journey together through the world created in the pages of a great book. Although readers enter the book together, the connections made are personal because each individual brings his or her own experiences to every story.

Great books connect with readers by pulling us into the pages, reminding us of events we've already experienced and allowing us to again experience them through another's eyes. Great books also take us to places we've never been, and in doing so, tempt or dissuade us from venturing there alone. Great books are a means of opening new worlds to children by providing examples of perspectives, problems, and imaginings they haven't encountered or even dreamed of. Above all, great books for first-grade children entertain, provide motivation for learning to read, and will keep them reading for a lifetime.

In a book-based classroom, a book isn't just read and put back on the shelf. It's read again and again. The 50 must-have books introduced in the following pages should be a part of every childhood. They should become dog-eared, marked with sticky notes, and referred to as examples of quality literature. The authors' names will become as common to your students as their best friends' names. The words, characters, and associated themes in each book will become the basis for learning across the curriculum.

The key to successful lessons for first graders is motivation. With motivation and examples of relevance to the real world, six-year-old students are more focused and better able to commit information to memory. In most of the lessons I teach, I can easily find motivation in the pages of a great book. These books supply evidence to children that words have meaning, writing is a task worthy of doing, reading is a skill worth learning, and math and science are occurrences that happen in the real world, not just in a classroom.

So find the must-have books in the pages that follow. Read them aloud with your first graders for pure entertainment value. Then revisit the books to link the learning of skills to a favorite character, idea, theme, or words taken from their pages. Experiment with the mini-lessons and activities in this book, and adapt them to suit your students' needs and your teaching style. Use some lessons and activities for your whole class and others for small-group instruction, or stretch some of them over the course of several days. However you present the ideas in this book, my hope is that together you and your students will enjoy a year of book-based learning.

A Few Words About the Read-Aloud and Rich Vocabulary Connection

It's no surprise that by their senior year, students at the top of their class know about four times as many words as their lower performing classmates. "Most chilling, however," write Beck, McKeown, and Kucan in *Bringing Words to Life* (pages 1–2), "is the finding that once established, such differences appear difficult to ameliorate. This is clearly very bad news!"

The good news is that implementing effective vocabulary instruction has become a priority in elementary schools. Techniques for providing the most effective and meaningful vocabulary instruction have also been identified. For first-grade teachers, the most appropriate place to begin is with a daily read-aloud, which gives the opportunity to teach one or two new words. Read-aloud time will provide a wealth of vocabulary words in meaningful contexts over the course of the school year.

In the pages of my book, I highlight one or more words from each of the 50 must-have read-aloud books. Activities and direct examples from my classroom illustrate how to best present words from trade books to help first graders commit new word knowledge to memory and to apply these newly discovered words in new situations.

When sharing a wordless picture book or discussing a simple, grade level text intended for independent reading, look for a prevailing theme or level-appropriate word to highlight for vocabulary instruction. In Mayer Mercer's *Frog, Where Are You?*, for example, a boy and his dog face numerous challenges when searching for Frog. The word *determined* is introduced as a rich vocabulary word for describing the characters' actions. The word and definition are reinforced in future retellings of the story.

Chapter 1:
Welcome Back to School!

10 Must-Have Books to Kick Off the School Year

Chapter Objectives:

* practicing speaking and listening skills
* increasing vocabulary awareness
* representing numbers from 1 to 20 with objects
* using conventions of spelling in written compositions
* using pictures and phonemic spelling to convey basic ideas
* using descriptive words and adjectives to convey basic ideas
* relating stories to personal experience
* kicking off the school year with great read-alouds with a school theme

In a perfect world, students would enter your classroom each fall filled with self-motivation and an eagerness to learn. The reality is that teachers need a little help in getting all their "ducks in a row" at the beginning of each new school year.

This chapter presents ten must-have books and activities to kick off a year of successful learning. Read aloud these great books and then let the characters, their problems, and ultimate solutions bring extra excitement to the often-mundane beginning of the year tasks.

Read about *Emily's First 100 Days of School* to show how important and fun numbers can be. Let students get to know the characters in *Miss Malarkey Doesn't Live in Room 10* and then get to know more about each other. Introduce *Yoko* during a read-aloud to help establish a classroom atmosphere that encourages students to be accepting of individual differences. *Chrysanthemum* can help children feel comfortable about sharing ideas. Use *Arthur's Teacher Trouble* to set up a spelling center. Students explore beginning letter sounds by writing poems to go with *Best Friends*. *Leo the Late Bloomer* will introduce the concept of setting goals to students. In *David Goes to School,* the main character teaches classroom rules by his own example, while Raymond in *Never Spit on Your Shoes* cautions first-day-of-school first-graders to, of course, never spit on their shoes. Spawn discussions about overcoming obstacles in learning with *Thank You, Mr. Falker.*

Read on for activities that will help you kick off a school year of book-based learning.

---

10 Must-Have Books to Kick Off the School Year

Emily's First 100 Days of School by Rosemary Wells

Miss Malarkey Doesn't Live in Room 10 by Judy Finchler

Yoko by Rosemary Wells

Chrysanthemum by Kevin Henkes

Arthur's Teacher Trouble by Marc Brown

Best Friends by Steven Kellogg

Leo the Late Bloomer by Robert Kraus

David Goes to School by David Shannon

Never Spit on Your Shoes by Denys Cazet

Thank You, Mr. Falker by Patricia Polacco

Emily's First 100 Days of School

by Rosemary Wells

LEARNING ABOUT Representing Numbers

"When I was little, in elementary school, math was no fun for me. It was taught by rote, and it was impossible for me to see how I would use these lessons in real life."

—From "Author's Note" in
Emily's First 100 Days of School

In this bright and lively book, Rosemary Wells sets out to prove that math can be fun and that math learning does translate to the real world. Emily leaves her mama's arms on the first day of school, too excited to cry, and meets her teacher, Miss Cribbage, who promises to throw a big party on the 100th day of school. As the days of school progress, Emily and her classmates meet numbers in situations they never imagined— or rather they did, but never gave a second thought to. The 76 trombones in the song and the 57 varieties on a pickle jar label help convince Emily and the other children that numbers are everywhere.

Once your students realize how meaningful the role of numbers is in our lives and how numbers sometimes appear when we least expect them, learning becomes more personal and more relevant than filling in the blanks on a worksheet. My first goal as a primary teacher at the beginning of the school year is to make learning math fun, hands-on, and meaningful. By

Rich Vocabulary

monitor *v.* to keep an eye on

counting buttons, candy corn, or even silver-painted popcorn chains instead of using rote pencil-and-paper counting, I also take the intimidation out of math. I introduce this approach to math in my classroom by simply stating three steps as follows:

1. Here's the skill we'll be learning about (counting, for example).
2. Here's one way this skill occurs in the real world (counting the days in school).
3. Here's how we'll explore it meaningfully (counting real objects).

In the mini-lesson that follows, the students and I set out to make number journals of our own and begin planning ahead for our own 100th Day of School party. In doing so, even the most "mathophobic" students agree that counting can be fun.

The day prior to the mini-lesson, we hold a math workshop where students produce large quantities of tens and ones for use throughout the school year to represent the numbers from 1 to 100. To incorporate the ideas depicted in *Emily's First 100 Days of School,* I set up stations where students make tens by placing 10 pieces of candy corn, 10 acorns or seeds, or 10 pennies into small paper ketchup cups marked TEN; attaching 10 similar-sized stickers (stars or flowers, for example) onto strips of adding machine paper; and rubber stamping pictures in rows of 10 on strips of adding machine paper. Students make ones by placing the

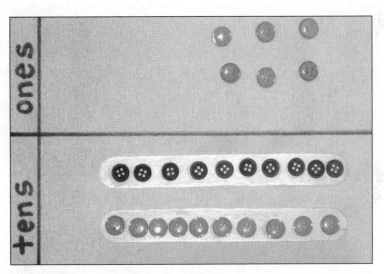

same kinds of objects in small paper ketchup cups marked ONES. They can also cut apart the strips of stickers and rubber-stamped pictures to make ones.

Note: In this mini-lesson, the students and I explore the numbers from 1 to 20. Adapt the lesson to accommodate the needs of your students and your learning goals. You may choose to repeat it throughout the year to reinforce the understanding of new decades of numbers.

Tens and ones made in Emily's math workshop

It's also fun to include *Emily's First 100 Days of School* as part of calendar time by rereading the page that corresponds to each new day of school.

Mrs. L.:	We've been keeping track of our days in school just like Emily's class does in *Emily's 100 Days of School*.
Kyle:	Today's our fifteenth day.
Mrs. L.:	That means we have eighty-five days till our Hundredth Day of School party. Listen to how Rosemary Wells describes numbers: "[Numbers] appear in our

games, in our poetry, and in songs. . . . Some numbers are so much a part of our language that certain things come to mind the moment the number is mentioned; other numbers are shy and need to be brought out of their hiding places. In this book all numbers are equally important, and all are fun." Today, we're going to have some fun with numbers. First tell me about a number that immediately makes you think of something when you hear it.

Emily:	When I hear "three," I think of "The Three Little Pigs."
Travis:	I think of "Three Blind Mice" or "The Three Bears."
Grace:	Twelve is a dozen, so I think of a dozen eggs when I see the number twelve.
Mrs. L.:	Great thinking! Rosemary Wells thinks of a dozen, too. She writes that Leo and Emily picked a dozen zinnias for Mama's birthday.
Casey:	I like the page with the song about ninety-nine bottles of pop on the wall.
Mrs. L.:	I do, too. I think it's clever how Rosemary Wells thought of a way to celebrate all the numbers from one to one hundred. Many numbers can be celebrated in obvious ways—like the twenty-six letters in the alphabet or the fifty stars on the American flag. But for a lot of other numbers, Rosemary Wells had to be creative—like the way Mama can count fifty-six ways she loves Emily off the top of her head, how Emily can read a book with forty-seven words all by herself, and how Leo can't see any of the eighty-nine calories in Aunt Mim's tomato soup.
Greg:	I remember that there are twenty-seven letters in the name of Emily's hometown. I remember because we counted the letters in our hometown, State College, and got twelve.
Mrs. L.:	Exactly. Today we're going to take a closer look at what a few other numbers look like. I've copied the numbers from one to twenty on cards and placed them in this bag. I'll call you to help me pick one number at a time. We'll build that number using the tens and ones we made in our math workshop.
Joey:	I counted LOTS of candy corn into counting cups.
Christy:	I made a hundred out of flower sticker-tens.
Mrs. L.:	These will come in handy. After we make each number with tens and ones, we'll think of the way it's used in a poem, a game or a song, as Rosemary Wells suggests. Josh, would you like to be the first one to choose a number?
Josh:	Sure—it's sixteen. I'll use candy corn to build the number. Here's one ten of candy corn, with six ones. That's sixteen.
Mrs. L.:	Nice work. Can you recall a song or a poem or another special way sixteen is used?
Casey:	Maybe you should check the book.
Mrs. L.:	Good idea! *(I begin to sing the song "16 Tons.")* "You load sixteen tons, what do you get?"
Daniel:	I've heard that song.
Grace:	My sister's sixteen.
Mrs. L.:	The number sixteen has special meaning for some of us. Let's try another number. Brooke, would you choose a number, please?

Brooke: It's fifteen. I'll make fifteen with the flower stamps. I'll use one ten and five ones.

Mrs. L.: Tell me something special about the number fifteen.

Jeannie: It's one less than sixteen.

Katie: I think my cat is fifteen.

William: In the book, fifteen is the one about fifteen horses swimming.

Mrs. L.: The boat's motor is fifteen horsepower. So, fifteen is special, too. Let's choose one more before I give you a chance to try this on your own. Travis, would you choose a number, please?

Travis: It's nine.

Greg: My brother will be nine on his birthday.

Maddie: I have nine stuffed animals on my shelf. I counted them last night when I was trying to go to sleep.

Josh: I wish I had nine cookies to eat—I'm hungry.

Travis: I made nine with the pennies: nine ones.

Mrs. L.: Nice work. In the book, there are nine planets in our solar system. As the book shows, numbers are everywhere—and they're an important part of our world. Without them, we wouldn't know how many things we needed at the grocery store, how fast to go, how old we are, how many minutes till bedtime—

Billy: Or how many minutes till lunch.

Sara: Or days till my birthday—mine is exactly twenty days away.

Joey: Or how many pennies are in my bank—I have at least eighty-nine, I bet.

Mrs. L.: I'd like to give you all a chance to show me how a number from one to twenty is special to you. I think we will probably agree with Rosemary Wells—numbers can be fun!

Grace: I think our Hundredth Day of School Party will be fun, too.

2 and 7 in our world

After the mini-lesson, I send students to their seats to work on a page for a class number journal. Using the same bag of numbers from our mini-lesson, students choose a number from 1 to 20 and write and illustrate that number on an index card. They work during free time at the math center to illustrate all the numbers from 1 to 20.

When all the numbers have been completed, we display the index cards in numerical order near the calendar where we keep track of the days in school. Each day at calendar time artists take turns introducing the Number of the Day and its special significance in our world.

10 Great Ways to Celebrate the 100th Day of School

1. Share 100 cupcakes (donated by parents).
2. Gather 100 children to sing "Happy 100th Day of School" (sung to the tune of "Happy Birthday to You").
3. Collect and count 100 objects from inside or outside the classroom.
4. Write your name 100 times (or count 100 kisses like Emily).
5. Reread *Emily's First 100 Days of School* by Rosemary Wells.
6. Measure 100 inches (or run a 100-yard dash).
7. Do something for 100 seconds (like standing on one foot like Roger did in the book).
8. Write 100 words in book-spelling.
9. Work in groups to glue together 100 Popsicle sticks (or bottle caps like Lewis did in the book).
10. Get together with book buddies to collectively read 100 books.

More Must-Have Books
To Kick Off the School Year

....

Miss Malarkey Doesn't Live in Room 10
by Judy Finchler

LEARNING ABOUT   ## Listening and Speaking Skills

Miss Malarkey doesn't live in room 10; she has just moved into the same apartment building as one of her first graders. This first-grade narrator sets out to prove that his teacher doesn't

live in room 10, but many classmates still have their doubts! Until Miss Malarkey moved, he and his classmates knew that the real reason students weren't allowed in the teachers' room was because the teachers didn't want students to see their messy room. And of course, the teachers eat dinner in the cafeteria and have recess in the gym before lining up to brush their teeth in the water fountain outside room 10.

Mrs. L.'s bag

To prove to my first graders that I don't live in room 4, I read *Miss Malarkey Doesn't Live in Room 10* and assure them that our teachers' room

is where we eat lunch— not sleep— and that after school, I eat dinner with my family at home and not in the cafeteria. I explain that after dinner I walk my dogs, Sydney and Jordan, and that I do not play in the gymnasium with the other teachers. To further prove my point and to let students get to know me a little better, I share a bag I've brought from home, which is packed with items that tell about me. I invite students to select items from the bag and guess what they tell about me.

After our discussion of the things that tell about me, students copy the following homework assignment onto a paper bag:

Homework

Find 3 things from home that tell about me.
Place the things in this bag and bring to school.

> ## Rich Vocabulary
>
> **misconception** *n.* an idea that is not true (It's a misconception that teachers live in their classrooms!)

The next day, we share students' items and get to know each other better. As each student shares his or her items, snap a picture to display on a Class Projects bulletin board. (Check out the dedication page of *Miss Malarkey Doesn't Live in Room 10* to see what Miss Malarkey's class project board looks like.) Or have students illustrate the items from home with captions under each item.

Yoko
by Rosemary Wells

Using Sound-Spelling To Convey Ideas

"What's in your lunch?" asked one of the Franks.
"Ick! It's green! It's seaweed!"
"Oh, no!" said the other Frank. "Don't tell me that's raw fish!"
"Watch out! It's moving!" said Doris.
"Yuck-o-rama!" said Tulip and Fritz.
   —From *Yoko*, pages 11–13

Yoko is a beautiful and sensitively written story that encourages the acceptance of individual differences. When it's time for lunch, Yoko's classmates' favorite things to eat range from a peanut butter and honey sandwich to an egg salad sandwich on pumpernickel to a meatball grinder. Despite this variety of food, Yoko's classmates are less than open to new culinary experiences.

So their teacher, Mrs. Jenkins, holds an International Food Day to celebrate different foods. There's not one nibble of nuts or sip of smoothie left—but no one has touched a piece of Yoko's sushi. Heartbroken, she sits under the Learning Tree bulletin board. Then she hears the clickety-click of chopsticks and sees Timothy trying to taste the sushi.

After reading the story and relating your students' individual

One of my favorite things is French fris with purple kachup

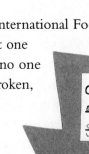

Leaves for our Learning Tree

One of my favorite things is a plat of sueshs and a dal of green tey ice cream.

Rich Vocabulary

fretted *v.* worried

differences to those of Mrs. Jenkins's, make a yearlong Learning
Tree bulletin board with a pencil trunk and
branches similar to the one shown on page 24 of
Yoko. To make this bulletin board interactive, display
students' photos around the perimeter of the
bulletin board. Have them match the photos to the
corresponding leaf on the learning tree.

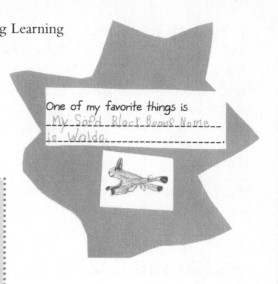

TEACHING TIP

Laminate leaves before students write on them and
use erasable markers for a year of learning leaves
that change to suit the needs and studies of your
class, for example, words with missing blend
sounds, homonyms, synonyms, and sums and
differences. Have a set of laminated student photos
on hand to keep track of whose turn it is to work
at different activities or for filling in class graphs.

Chrysanthemum
by Kevin Henkes

LEARNING ABOUT

Speaking and Listening Rules

*During naptime, Victoria raised her hand and informed Mrs. Chud that
Chrysanthemum's name was spelled with* thirteen *letters.*

   "That's exactly half as many letters as there are in the entire
*alphabet!" Victoria explained. "Thank you for sharing that with us,
Victoria," said Mrs. Chud. "Now put your head down."*

Taking turns sharing ideas at the appropriate time is a worthy task to
model with first graders. Use the situations and words of the characters
in *Chrysanthemum* to lay the groundwork for sharing ideas in a classroom
situation. In the above example from the book, Victoria raises her hand
to talk, which is an appropriate first step when speaking in class, but
should she be talking about the number of letters in Chrysanthemum's
name during naptime? Definitely not.

Rich Vocabulary
dreadful *adj.* awful, terrible
humorous; *adj.* funny

Outline the procedure below for sharing and listening to ideas in a group.

When Sharing Ideas
1. Make sure what you are going to say adds to the discussion.
2. Raise your hand before speaking.
3. Wait for your classmates to pay attention.
4. Speak slowly and clearly.

When Listening to Others
1. Look at the speaker.
2. Fold your hands in your lap.
3. Listen carefully.
4. Wait to share your own ideas until the speaker has finished talking.

Hold a discussion of the number of letters in names, the origins of names, or a *Chrysanthemum* book discussion so students can practice sharing their ideas and listening to others.

Arthur's Teacher Trouble
by Marc Brown

 **LEARNING ABOUT**

Print and Spelling Conventions

The next day, Mr. Ratburn announced a spelling test for Friday. "I want you to study very hard,"
he said. "The test will have a hundred words." Buster looked pale. "And," continued Mr. Ratburn,
"the two students with the highest scores will represent our class at the all-school spellathon." That
week everyone in Arthur's class studied harder than ever.
— From *Arthur's Teacher Trouble,* pages 12–14

Build good spelling habits in your students that they will have fun practicing from the start of the new school year. Whether you use weekly spelling lists, sound-spelling, or unit-related words, an area designated as Arthur's spelling center is a great place for students to get hands-on practice with words in isolation. Introduce the following materials one or a few at a time depending on your class needs and abilities:

Arthur's Spelling Center Materials
- magnetic letters and boards

Rich Vocabulary

grumble *v.* to complain in an angry way

Teaching With Favorite Read-Alouds in First Grade

- basket of foam letters
- cardboard letters in envelopes
- individual pocket charts for displaying letters
- white boards and dry-erase markers
- individual-sized chalkboards and chalk (Use paint brushes dipped in water on these boards for a fun change of pace.)
- alphabet stamps and stamp pads
- alphabet stencils
- typewriter or computer
- transparent highlighting tape to use in selected books

Be sure to place a copy of *Arthur's Teacher Trouble* in the center to remind students of Arthur's victory at the all-school spellathon.

---

5 Great Ideas for Extra-Special Spelling Practice

1. **Laptop Words:** Students type words onto a laptop computer that is attached to a printer.

2. **Crayon Resist Words:** Students write words on white paper with a white crayon and then paint over the words with watercolor paints.

3. **Rainbow Words:** Students use crayons to completely color an index card in rainbow colors (pressing firmly with crayons). Then they color over rainbow colors with black crayon. Students use Popsicle sticks to write words, which appear in rainbow colors on a black background. **Note:** Art Scratch Paper can be purchased that is ready to write on from art and school supply stores.

4. **Sparkly 3-D Words:** After you mix equal parts of white glue and sparkly toothpaste, students write words with Q-Tip pencils.

5. **Messy Words With Finger Pencils:** Students form words after dipping their fingers in shaving cream (or finger paints).

Best Friends
by Steven Kellogg

 **LEARNING ABOUT** ## Using Descriptive Words

Later I heard Mrs. Jenkins say that Louise had made lots of new friends and was having the best summer of her life. It wasn't fair. She wasn't lonely like me. She wasn't missing me at all. Louise Jenkins was a traitor! She was my worst friend. I wished a volcanic eruption would blast Pine Cone Peak into pebbles.
— From *Best Friends,* pages 12–13

Wishing a volcanic eruption would blast your best friend's mountain resort into pebbles isn't exactly the way we think best friends should behave—or is it? Let Steven Kellogg's best friends, Louise Jenkins and

Rich Vocabulary

contagious *adj.* something that is spread to others

Kathy Cotski, show students how even the closest of friends have problems and difficult feelings to work out. Kathy and Louise prove that true best friends remain friends through it all.

Share the story, and then discuss the range of emotions Kathy experiences throughout the story—from best friends to worst friends; from jealous, awful, and lonely to happy, sharing and caring.

Then write each of the letters in BEST FRIENDS on an index card. Pair students, and distribute one card to each pair to list the qualities of friends—B is for Being there, E is for Explaining things, S is for Special friends and times, T is for Trying together, and so on. Display these phonemic poems as reminders of what it takes to be a good friend. Refer to the ideas often as your class begins a new year of establishing new and maintaining old friendships.

Being there
Explaning things
Speshol friends and time's
Tring togrer thrustfl
Fuoreis Fihting
Respecked
Imposobol to brack up
Ecxlent memrees
Neis
Diserhens
Sharing

Best Friends poem

Leo the Late Bloomer
by Robert Kraus

Leo couldn't do anything right. He couldn't read. He couldn't write. He couldn't draw. He was a sloppy eater. And he never said a word. . . . Then one day, in his own good time, Leo bloomed!
—From *Leo the Late Bloomer,* pages 5–11, 24

When Leo's mother assures her husband that their son Leo is just a late bloomer, he thinks, *Better late than never.* First-grade teachers often take comfort in this philosophy when it comes to waiting for students to form letters correctly and neatly, use conventional spelling, and develop reading fluency. "Better late than never" is certainly a legitimate feeling for teachers and parents, but it's also important to stress to students the idea that, like Leo, we all reach certain learning goals in our own good time. Take the opportunity to point out how important it would be to Leo to have his friends offer patience, understanding, and support as he works on learning to read, write, and draw. Remind students that, like Leo, we all work on and accomplish different things at different times.

Rich Vocabulary

troubled *adj.* worried

Introduce beginning-of-the-year goal setting after reading *Leo the Late Bloomer*. Have each student think of a goal to work on, and then brainstorm ways to reach that goal. Here's a sample from my classroom.

Name: Grace

My goal is: to put better spaces between my words when writing.

Here's how I will work on this goal: put two fingers between each of my words.

....

David Goes to School
by David Shannon

 **LEARNING ABOUT** **Classroom Rules**

David's teacher always said . . . NO, DAVID! No yelling. No pushing. No running in the halls.
— From *David Goes to School*, page 1

Poor David. He's in trouble—again. This time he's having difficulty following the school rules. Most first-grade children will sympathize with David's lack of control in raising his hand to talk, paying attention, and waiting his turn. The words, childlike printing on primary writing paper, and illustrated with David Shannon's simple drawings, make this story even more realistic. First graders have fun rereading the simple text using the picture clues—and imitating a teacher voice with lots of expression, of course.

This book provides lots of room for a discussion of how David should behave in school. Let his problems influence the creation of your own set of classroom rules. Stated positively, the rules might look something like the ones shown below.

1. Walk in school.
2. Be polite.
3. Raise your hand to talk.
4. Keep your hands (and feet) to yourself.
5. Be a good listener.
6. Take turns.
7. Respect each other and classroom property.

Also discuss suitable consequences for not obeying the rules and possible rewards for following them.

> # Rich Vocabulary
>
> **disrupt** *v.* to cause an interruption; to disturb

Never Spit on Your Shoes
by Denys Cazet

LEARNING ABOUT | **Using Sound-Spelling**

As Arnie sits down with a cold glass of milk and a plate of cookies, he begins to recount his first day of first grade to his mother—although he leaves out a few details. But like most parents, Arnie's mother can read between the lines. With an uncanny understanding of what goes on in a typical first-grade classroom, Denys Cazet's illustrations reveal the details to readers. From the little guy with untied shoelaces and a note stuck on his back who says, "Thank you for inviting me but I think I'll be going home now" to the little bunny showing off a pair of new shoes and making a pair of paper chain earrings, these are real first-grade characters. And there's the new student, Raymond, who can write his name backwards. When Raymond needs a little help counting to 16, Arnie lends him a hand—and a few toes—by removing his clothes to count toes with Raymond. Of course, it's Raymond who suggests, "you never spit on your shoes" for a class rule.

> ### Rich Vocabulary
> **slumped** *v.* bent over

The detailed and comical illustrations in this book are wonderful inspirations for first graders' first-day memoirs. Close to the end of the first day of school, I ask students to recall their favorite events of the day in a detailed illustration. I then ask students to label their drawings, encouraging them to use sound-spelling. Some students may write phrases or sentences, while others may dictate their captions. This activity helps you assess where students are in their writing and spelling development. Collect, date, and save these first-day treasures in portfolios. Students will be able to see how their writing improves from the first day of school throughout the year.

Note: You may adapt this activity for use later in the school year.

"My favorite part (of the first day) was making new friends." — Christy

Thank You, Mr. Falker

by Patricia Polacco

 **Relating Stories to Personal Experience**

The grandpa held the jar of honey so that all the family could see, then dipped a ladle into it and drizzled honey on the cover of a small book.

The little girl had just turned five.

"Stand up, little one," he cooed. "I did this for your mother, your uncles, your older brother, and now you."

Then he handed the book to her. "Taste!"

She dipped her finger into the honey and put it into her mouth.

"What is that taste?" the grandma asked.

The little girl answered, "Sweet!"

Then all of the family said in a single voice, "Yes, and so is knowledge, but knowledge is like the bee that made that sweet honey, you have to chase it through the pages of a book!"

The little girl knew that the promise to read was at last hers. Soon she was going to read.

— From *Thank You, Mr. Falker,* page 7

If only learning to read could be like taking a lick of honey. As Trisha, the main character in this story, and so many others know, it is a much more difficult task. *Thank You, Mr. Falker* is one of the most touching children's stories I have ever read; most teachers can only hope to have the kind of life-changing impact on the life of a child that the real Mr. Falker had on Patricia Polacco, the real Trisha.

Reading about young Trisha curled up in her hiding place to escape the hurtful comments being hurled at her because of a learning disability is heartbreaking. Realizing that she overcame a great obstacle with the help of Mr. Faulker and grew up to be a very talented writer and illustrator is heartening. Knowing that Trisha had the opportunity to thank Mr. Falker thirty years after the fact and tell him of her success is awesome.

Share this story to encourage all those children who, like Patricia Polacco, don't see letters and numbers the way they are usually processed. Discuss the hard work involved in overcoming a great obstacle and how Patricia Polacco actually went on to use the very same skill she struggled to learn in earning a living.

Talk about Trisha's feelings throughout the story, how those who teased her probably felt about themselves, and the importance of respecting and supporting each other's differences. Help students make personal connections to the text by using tell-me discussion statements such as the following:

> ## Rich Vocabulary
>
> **announced** *v.* said out loud; told

Tell Me About *Thank You, Mr. Falker*

1. Tell me about Trisha's feelings when:
   - Grandpa gave her the book with the drop of honey on it.
   - first grade ended and she still couldn't read.
   - she was alone in the reader called *Our Neighborhood*.
   - Mr. Falker held up one of her pictures in front of the class and called it "absolutely brilliant."
   - Eric found her in her hiding place.
   - she was asked to read in front of the class before Mr. Falker and Miss Plessy worked with her.
   - she read her first sentence to the class after she learned to read.

2. Tell me what you think about Patricia Polacco's dedication to the real Mr. Falker who "will forever be my hero."

3. Tell me about a hero of yours.

4. Tell me how Mr. Falker must have felt when he:
   - heard Trisha read a paragraph for the first time.
   - marched Eric to the principal's office.
   - learned that Patricia Polacco writes children's books for a living.
   - read *Thank You, Mr. Falker.*

5. Tell me why Patricia Polacco drew a picture of the classic *Great Expectations* by Charles Dickens on the dedication page.

6. Tell me about a time you cried happy tears like Mr. Falker and Miss Plessy did when Trisha read her first sentence.

7. Tell me about a time you felt you couldn't do something.

Other Must-Have Books by Patricia Polacco

My Rotten Redheaded Older Brother

Picnic at Mudsock Meadow

Just Plain Fancy

The Keeping Quilt

The Bee Tree

Babushka Baba Yaga

Some Birthday!

Mrs. Katz and Tush

My Ol' Man

Thunder Cake

Chapter 2: Let's Celebrate!
10 Must-Have Books for Rainy Days, Birthdays, and Other Special Days

Chapter Objectives:
* ✷ practicing speaking and listening skills
* ✷ creating and continuing patterns
* ✷ reading familiar stories with fluency and expression
* ✷ making inferences
* ✷ identifying problems in stories
* ✷ writing in a variety of genres
* ✷ using descriptive language to add details to written work
* ✷ relating stories to personal experience
* ✷ increasing vocabulary awareness
* ✷ celebrating special days with special read-alouds

We all know what it's like in a first-grade classroom the day before winter vacation, the day of a birthday party, or even the first snowy day of winter—the smallest disruption can wreak havoc on the productivity level of the classroom. Special days call for special read-alouds.

This chapter is all about great books and activities to focus excited first-graders' energy. Take students' minds off of spring's first thunderstorm with a lesson on vowel sounds based on *Thunder Cake. Jimmy's Boa and the Big Splash Birthday Bash* will have students eager to write their own party invitations. Use *A Weekend with Wendell* to sharpen your class's inference skills. After sharing *Arthur's Birthday*, let children write birthday letters. Hold an art show to display work inspired by a reading (and viewing) of *The Art Lesson*.

Owl Moon will spark students' interest in descriptive writing. Let *The Night Tree* be the basis for an activity on creating patterns. Every student will be able to relate to Alexander's feelings in *Alexander and the Terrible, Horrible, No Good, Very Bad Day*. With the help of *The Polar Express*, increase students' reading fluency. Encourage some list writing after reading *Song and Dance Man*.

Read aloud one of the must-have books in this chapter, and turn any day into a special day.

---

10 Must-Have Books for Rainy Days, Birthdays, and Other Special Days

Thunder Cake by Patricia Polacco

Jimmy's Boa and the Big Splash Birthday Bash by Trinka Hakes Noble

A Weekend with Wendell by Kevin Henkes

Arthur's Birthday by Marc Brown

The Art Lesson by Tomie dePaola

Owl Moon by Jane Yolen

Night Tree by Eve Bunting

Alexander and the Terrible, Horrible, No Good, Very Bad Day by Judith Viorst

The Polar Express by Chris Van Allsburg

Song and Dance Man by Karen Ackerman

Thunder Cake

by Patricia Polacco

LEARNING ABOUT Vowel Sounds

In my primary class each year, I always have at least one student who gets a bit trembly-lipped when the April sky darkens and a thunderstorm nears Pine Grove Mountain. Share *Thunder Cake* as a read-aloud in early spring—thunder cake season—to help children face this common childhood fear.

Prior to the read-aloud, I conduct a thunderstorm survey. Duplicate the reproducible on page 38. Cut out and distribute the survey question. Sort the responses into groups according to the circled number, and chart the results as shown below.

not scared at all	1	2	3	4	5	6	7	8	9	10	really scared
	7	5	1		2	2		2			

Our read-aloud begins with a discussion of our class's feelings about thunderstorms based on the data gathered in our survey.

And, since several students always ask to copy the thunder cake recipe from the last page of the book, I decided to turn the request into a word study lesson on long vowels. I copied the recipe onto chart paper, deleting some of the long vowel sounds. A reproducible of this recipe appears on page 39.

Rich Vocabulary

cooed *v.* said in a sweet voice

scurried *v.* moved quickly

Mrs. L.: From the results of our *Thunder Cake* survey, I'd say none of you would be hiding under the bed during a thunderstorm.

Maddie: Patricia Polacco did when she was little.

Mrs. L.: If my dog, Sydney, could participate in the survey, she'd circle a ten with her paw. At the first sound of thunder, even miles away, Sydney hides under the coffee table.

Grace:	My sister sits on my mom's lap and hides her eyes.
Josh:	My little brother cries.
Mrs. L.:	I wish there was a way to make Sydney and others feel less afraid.
Casey:	You could give her a piece of thunder cake. Do you think eating it would help?
Daniel:	No. Her grandma made her help with the thunder cake to prove how brave she was.
Emily:	She had to get the eggs from old Nellie Peck Hen.
Sara:	And milk from the Kicking Cow.
Makenzie:	She also climbed the ladder to get the tomatoes—
Katie:	And she went through the woods—
Peter:	Tangleweed Woods—
Katie:	—to get to the shed.
Mrs. L.:	Whether you're afraid of thunder or not, making a thunder cake sounds fun and delicious—a nice rainy day activity to do with an adult.
Grace:	Do you have the recipe?
Mrs. L.:	I do.
Josh:	Could I have it, please? I want to make a thunder cake for my little brother next time there's a thunderstorm. He'd circle a ten like Sydney if he could.
Joey:	I think I might be allergic to thunder cake. Are there really tomatoes in it?
Mrs. L.:	You're about to find out. I've written the recipe for you to copy and take home. But, there's one problem. *(I display the recipe.)*
Joey:	You skipped some letters when you wrote it.
Mrs. L.:	Yes, I did. I left out the letters that make some long vowel sounds.
Casey:	Maybe they're hiding because they're afraid of thunder.
Mrs. L.:	Let's find them and put them back in the recipe. Without these long vowels, the recipe is missing something.
Brooke:	How will we know what's missing if we don't know what the words are supposed to be?
Mrs. L.:	What clues do we have?
Sara:	Some of the letters are already there.
Mrs. L.:	Right. We have beginning letter clues to help us. What kind of words are we looking for?
Emily:	It's a recipe so they'll be cooking words.
Mrs. L.:	Right! The words with missing letters will all be in the context of a recipe so that's the kind of words we need to be thinking about. Let's try the first word. What sounds are already there?
Jacob:	*C-r-m.*
Mrs. L.:	Now look at the next word.
Class:	*Together.*
Madeline:	Cr_ _ m together.
Mrs. L.:	Read the rest of the line.
Class:	"One at a t_ m_."

Katie:	Time! "One at a time" makes sense, and it's missing the *i*.
Jeannie:	Add a silent *e* at the end to make the *i* say its name.
Mrs. L.:	Excellent! Please add these letters for us, Jeannie, while the rest of us fill in the word *time* on our recipe cards. Cr_ _m together, one at a time . . .
Greg:	Cream together?
Mrs. L.:	Yes! When you mix ingredients with butter or shortening, you cream them. In this recipe, shortening is used. What two letters work together in the word *cream* to make the long *e* sound?
Peter:	*E* is first. Is the next letter *a* since *cream* rhymes with *dream*?
Mrs. L.:	That's wise thinking. Rhyming words are an excellent way to help with book-spelling. Peter, will you add the missing letters to the word *cream*, please, while the rest add it to recipe cards?
Daniel:	I know the next word is *tablespoon*. That's how much vanilla you need to add.
Mrs. L.:	Let's see if *tablespoon* fits.
Daniel:	It's a long *a* word.
Katie:	But you need a *b* and an *l* for *tablespoon*, and there aren't enough spaces.
Vince:	Maybe it's a teaspoon. That's a long *e* word. I bet it's *e* with *a* again.
Sara:	That fits!
Mrs. L.:	I see the word *teaspoon* again with missing letters.
Christy:	Me, too.
Mrs. L.:	Let's fill those in now. Christy, would you help us, please? It looks like the next ingredient we need is—
Class:	Eggs.
Bobby:	We have to sep-ar-ate them.
Mrs. L.:	Good reading. What do we separate?
Brooke:	The white part from the orange part. The orange part is the yolk. I've helped my mom separate eggs—it's hard to do.
Mrs. L.:	It looks like we add the yolks first. Then what?
Maddie:	The *wh* word is *whites*. That's the part of the egg that's left after you take away the yolks.
Joey:	I bet you beat the whites. *Beat* is another *e-a* word. I'll fill it in.
Mrs. L.:	Thanks, Joey. What letters are missing from *whites*?
Joey:	The *i*. Since the other missing letter is at the end of the word, I bet this is a silent *e* word, too. Silent *e* makes long vowel words.
Mrs. L.:	After that we add cold water and . . .
Class:	Tomatoes!
William:	Tomatoes has *toes* in it! The missing letters are *o* and *e*.
Mrs. L.:	Good work, William.
Casey:	I didn't know *tomato* ended in a silent *e*.
Mrs. L.:	It doesn't. *T-o-m-a-t-o* spells *tomato*. But when you add an *s* to show more than one, you add an *e* at the end before you add the *s*. Up to this point in the recipe for thunder cake, we've had to follow two long vowel rules. Tell me about these rules.

Josh:	There are the silent *e* words. A silent *e* can make long vowels.
Mrs. L.:	Right. When a word ends in silent *e*, the other vowel in the word is usually . . .
Class:	Long.
Mrs. L.:	Right. The vowel says its name. We've also discovered another long vowel rule.
Grace:	When there are two vowels together, one of the vowels is long.
Mrs. L.:	Yes. Is the first or the second vowel long?
Grace:	Umm . . . the first one?
Mrs. L:	Here's how I remember the "two vowels walking" rule.

> *When two vowels go walking,*
> *the first one does the talking,*
> *the second one does the walking.*

Let's write examples of this recipe for long vowels on the back of our thunder cake recipe before we continue.

Students choose a silent *e* word and a "two vowels walking" word to illustrate on the back of their reproducibles.

Depending on their interest, we either continue filling in the missing long vowels together or partners finish the recipe as an independent practice activity. As students work, I pass out store-bought thunder cookies as a special treat.

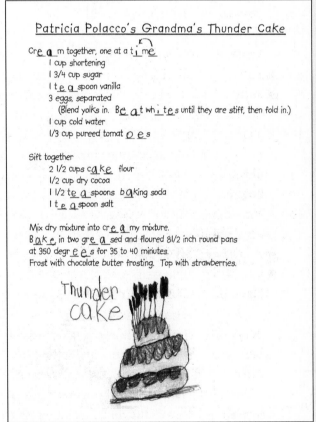

Thunder cake recipe

Long vowel recipe

More Must-Have Books for Rainy Days, Birthdays, and Other Special Days

Jimmy's Boa and the Big Splash Birthday Bash
by Trinka Hakes Noble

 **LEARNING ABOUT** **Writing Invitations**

Trinka Hakes Noble and illustrator Steven Kellogg keep kids tuned in and their imaginations running wild as Jimmy's birthday party at Sealand turns into a mad chain of events that eventually lands not only a boa but also an octopus and an assortment of goldfish at Jimmy's table for cake and ice cream.

After sharing this story for a read-aloud, give students practice writing in a different form by setting up an invitation writing center. Introduce the center by discussing the necessary information that must be included in an invitation. Chart the following questions to display in the center: *Who is having the party? What kind of party is it? When is the party? (date and time) Where is the party?*

For their invitations, have students draw an exciting picture based on Steven Kellogg's illustrations.

MORE FUN WITH THE BOOK

Set up an art center where students can shape Jimmy's boa out of clay (preferably forming clay). In the story, the boa is seen in a variety of situations and postures—wrapped around a shark's mouth, posing as a Sealand water slide for the kids, saving Jimmy's mom when she falls in the tank, and even making friends with an octopus. Have students use their imaginations to wrap their clay boas around objects such as pencils, books, cups, or erasers. Allow the boas to dry around the objects so they will permanently take the different shapes. Students can paint their boas with wild orange, green and yellow spots to resemble the book's friendly and helpful reptile.

Josh's party invitation

Rich Vocabulary

sensible *adj.* uses good thinking

A Weekend with Wendell

by Kevin Henkes

LEARNING ABOUT

Making Inferences

*When they pretended they worked in a bakery,
Wendell was the baker and Sophie was a sweet roll.
"Isn't this fun?" said Wendell.
Sophie didn't say anything.*
— From *A Weekend with Wendell*, pages 9

Sophie doesn't have to say anything. The illustration depicts her sitting on a bench in the corner—as a sweet roll—facing the wall. Wendell is wearing a chef's cap and smock, holding a wooden spoon, and dancing around. The picture speaks louder than words: Sophie is fed-up. But the tables turn when Sophie becomes a fire hydrant and Wendell is a burning building.

After a rainy-day read-aloud of *A Weekend with Wendell*, give students practice in making inferences based on visual clues in the story. Create sentences to match the illustrations of Sophie's expressions in the book, and write them on sentence strips. Here are some sentences I've used with my students.

Sophie "Says"—Without Words

*No, I did not make that mess!
I'm so upset, I can't even look at Wendell!
We're having fun now!
I'm not sure if I want to spend the weekend with Wendell.
Wendell, I could use a little help . . .
Mom! Come quick! I'm scared!
Ouch! That hurt!*

Have students take turns reading the sentences and then locating the corresponding illustrations in the book.

> ## Rich Vocabulary
>
> **annoy** *v.* to bother

ON ANOTHER DAY

Encourage students to take turns acting out parts of the story where words don't spell it out for the reader and pictures tell the story. Invite teams of volunteers to use facial expressions to act out these scenes for the rest of the class. If time allows, ask students to invent their own mini-scenes based on Sophie and Wendell.

Arthur's Birthday
by Marc Brown

Writing A Letter

"I can't wait! I can't wait!" said Arthur. "Are you sure it's only Tuesday?"
"See for yourself," said Mother.
"Four more days until my birthday!" said Arthur.
— From *Arthur's Birthday,* pages 3–4

Our Arthur's Birthday Celebration Area

Like most first graders, Arthur checks the calendar regularly to count the days until his birthday. Birthdays are extra fun in school—especially when they're celebrated with Marc Brown's Arthur.

For an Arthur-themed birthday celebration, make a bulletin board that features a smiling Arthur and his birthday cake with eight candles—just right for those first graders who turn seven with one candle to grow on—like the cover of *Arthur's Birthday.* Hang construction-paper birthday balloons with the names of students and their birth dates above Arthur.

I create a birthday box by wrapping a box with a removable lid in birthday paper. Then I fill it with birthday pencils and hats and Happy Birthday certificates for each birthday student, and copies of Arthur books for the student to select for a special birthday read-aloud. The other students make birthday cards with a friendly letter inside for the birthday student during free time on the day of the celebration. Have folded construction-paper cards, scrap paper, and markers available. Collect the cards, and tie them with a ribbon. Place them inside the birthday box to present during the party.

Rich Vocabulary

tradition *n.* something that is done the same way over and over again

Suggested Arthur Books To Include in the Birthday Box

Arthur Writes a Story
Arthur's Nose
Arthur's Underwear
Arthur's Eyes
Arthur's Puppy
Arthur's Tooth
Arthur's First Sleepover
Arthur Baby-sits
Arthur's TV Trouble
Arthur's Teacher Trouble
Arthur's Baby
Arthur's Hiccups

The Art Lesson
by Tomie dePaola

 **LEARNING ABOUT**

Preparing Work For Display

Tommy put his pictures up on the walls of his half of the bedroom. His mom put them up all around the house. His dad took them to the barbershop where he worked. Tom and Nana, Tommy's Irish grandfather and grandmother, had his pictures in their grocery store. Nana-Fall-River, his Italian grandmother, put one in a special frame on the table next to the photograph of Aunt Clo in her wedding dress.
— From *The Art Lesson,* pages 7–11

It's important for students to have a place where their work can be displayed on an ongoing basis. From artwork and writers' workshop stories to math and science recording sheets, students need a place in the classroom where they can "publish" their work and take ownership of the space. Based on the idea that Tomie dePaola's work was proudly shown at an early age, give your young artists a place to display their work in a variety of ways for friends.

Read aloud *The Art Lesson,* and then let Tomie dePaola's childhood drawings inspire an art lesson. Tommy draws and draws and draws. He draws pictures of his house, his room, his friends, animals, trucks, and even his teacher. Tommy's work proves that the more you practice, the better you become. Encourage students to illustrate similar objects using crayons, markers, watercolors, or whatever medium you desire. When they claim to be finished, ask them to revisit their work, to add details to "fill in all the white space." This editing should also include a sentence describing the work and giving it a title.

Just as Tomie dePaola's family displayed his drawings in a variety of places, display student artwork in special places in the classroom and around the school.

Knowing there will be an audience for their work can do wonders for your young artists. They will take extra care that will be evident in their final products.

Suggestions for Displaying Student Work

1. Hang a heavy cord or wire from two walls in your classroom. Attach clothespins labeled with individual student's names to hang work. (Glue names using *ABC* pasta shapes for fun.)
2. Have each student decorate a cardboard frame using pattern block cutouts, ribbon, tissue paper, buttons, sequins, glitter glue, and so on. Designate a part of the classroom or a bulletin board to display work.
3. Think about expanding display opportunities. If your writers' workshop stories are based on a favorite book or character, ask your librarian to display your class's work in the library. Making posters for healthy eating? Ask the cafeteria staff to display the posters for students to enjoy during lunch.

> ## Rich Vocabulary
>
> **talented** *adj.* to be particularly good at something

4. Establish a Students of the Month bulletin board in a central location at the school. Ask other teachers to include selected student work where visitors and other school personnel can see the wide variety of activities and accomplishments at the school.

5. Improve public relations while giving students a different audience for their work by enlisting the help of a parent or a friend with a store or business where work can be displayed.

....
Owl Moon
by Jane Yolen

LEARNING ABOUT

Using Descriptive Language

When you go owling you don't need words or warm or anything but hope.
That's what Pa says. The kind of hope that flies on silent wings
under a shining Owl Moon.
— From *Owl Moon,* page 32

Owl Moon is the perfect read-aloud for a snowy winter day. Every time I read this book, I am in awe of Jane Yolen's ability to take me owling: to make me feel the cold like someone's icy hand palm down my back, to see the snow whiter than the milk in a cereal bowl, and to hear feet crunching over the crisp snow and the contrasting dreamlike stillness of the owl-moon night. My copy of this Caldecott Medal book is marked with sticky notes highlighting favorite sentences.

Owl Moon is a perfect book for showing how expert authors paint pictures with words and how, with a little practice, first graders can, too. On a winter day, read aloud the book. Ask students to stop you when they hear a sentence that paints a picture with words. Write the sentences on a poster for reference during writing time.

Painting Pictures with the Words from *Owl Moon*
"The trees stood still as giant statues."
"And the moon was so bright the sky seemed to shine."
"Pa made a long shadow, but mine was short and round."
"We reached the line of pine trees, black and pointy against the sky."
"The moon made his face into a silver mask."
"The shadows were the blackest things I had ever seen. They stained the white snow."
"[The moon] seemed to fit exactly over the center of the clearing and the snow below it was whiter than the milk in a cereal bowl."
"Then the owl pumped its great wings and lifted off the branch like a shadow without a sound."

Rich Vocabulary

anticipate *v.* to wait anxiously for something to happen

We also expand simple sentences to paint pictures with words.

1. I like snowy days.
2. I like snowy days when the snow falls for hours.
3. I like snowy days when the snow falls for hours and piles up like a white blanket.
4. I like snowy days when the snow falls for hours and piles up like a white blanket outside my window.
5. I like snowy days when the snow falls for hours and piles up like a freshly washed white blanket outside my kitchen window.

MORE FUN WITH THE BOOK

Here's another activity to introduce after reading aloud *Owl Moon*. Students are always eager to paint their own pictures with words in writers' workshop stories.

Painting Pictures With Our Words

My fingers were as cold as a Popsicle. (Casey)

The snow looked like marshmallows falling on the ground. (Vince)

My red sled was scary-fast. (Peter)

The white kitten was invisible in the snow. (Christy)

(For more descriptive language practice, see Chapter 4 of *Literature-Based Mini-Lessons to Teach Writing* by Susan Lunsford, Scholastic Professional Books, 1998.)

Night Tree
by Eve Bunting

LEARNING ABOUT

Creating 3- and 4-Step Patterns

"Can I put on the popcorn chain?" Nina asks. She hops up and down and right out of one of her boots. Mom helps her get it back on.

Nina takes one end of the chain and I take the other and we wind it around our tree. We've brought apples and tangerines with strings on them, and we hang them from the branches. It's hard to hang string loops when you have gloves on, but it's too cold to take them off.

— From *Night Tree*, pages 17–18

Like Nina who hops up and down and right out of one of her boots, first graders are bustling with excited energy on snowy days and on days prior to holidays. Make the most of these days with Eve Bunting's *Night Tree*.

Rich Vocabulary

lopsided *adj.*
crooked; off to one side

Teaching With Favorite Read-Alouds in First Grade

After read-aloud, let students make their own *Night Tree* chains to hang as decorations on a night tree at home. This patterning activity is sure to soothe the excited six- and seven-year-olds in your class.

Cut a 15-inch length of string for each student, and supply cereals with holes such as Cheerios or Fruit Loops (no needles required). Students create 3-4 step patterns on the string with cereal.

Some Night Tree Patterns
- red loop, red loop, blue loop, Cheerio, red loop, red loop, blue loop, Cheerio . . .
- Cheerio, Cheerio, yellow loop, Cheerio, Cheerio, yellow loop . . .
- orange loop, Cheerio, red loop, orange loop, Cheerio, red loop, orange loop . . .
- red loop, red loop, green loop, green loop, red loop, red loop, green loop, green loop . . .
- Cheerio, red loop, Cheerio, green loop, Cheerio, red loop, Cheerio, green loop . . .

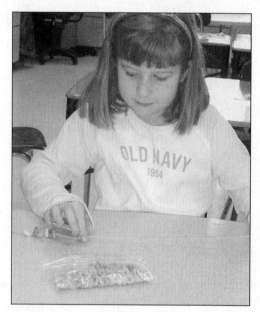

Night Tree cereal chains

Consider adopting a tree on school property and giving local birds a snowy day treat. (**Note**: Remind students to collect strings from the trees once the treats have been enjoyed by the animals.)

(For more fun with Eve Bunting's *Night Tree*, see *100 Skill-Building Lessons Using Ten Favorite Books* by Susan Lunsford, Scholastic Professional Books, 2001.)

Alexander and the Terrible, Horrible, No Good, Very Bad Day
by Judith Viorst

LEARNING ABOUT **Relating to Main Characters**

At school Mrs. Dickens liked Paul's picture of the sailboat better than my picture of the invisible castle. At singing time she said I sang too loud. At counting time she said I left out sixteen. Who needs sixteen? I could tell it was going to be a terrible, horrible, no good, very bad day.

— From *Alexander and the Terrible, Horrible, No Good, Very Bad Day*, pages 10–11

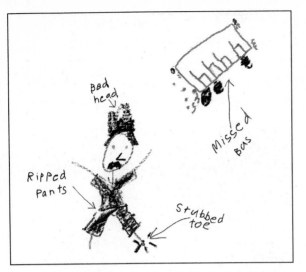

Greg's Terrible, Horrible, No Good, Very Bad Day

As Alexander's mother reminds him, "Some days are like that. Even in Australia." But when you're in the midst of a terrible, horrible, no good, very bad day, this sentiment offers little comfort. Sometimes the best thing to do is muddle through like Alexander, go to sleep (even if it means doing so with a burned-out Mickey Mouse night light and a bitten tongue), knowing that tomorrow has got to be a better day.

The picture on the cover of the book shows a defeated Alexander preparing to put the miserable day behind him. Let Ray Cruz's detailed drawings inspire the artists in your class to draw self-portraits of themselves having a terrible, horrible, no good very bad day. Is gum stuck in their hair? Do they have a Band-aid on their foreheads? Is there a tear in a favorite pair of pants? Did somebody else use all the syrup on their waffles? Students can label the atrocities of their day in their self-portraits and then share all the heart-wrenching events in small groups.

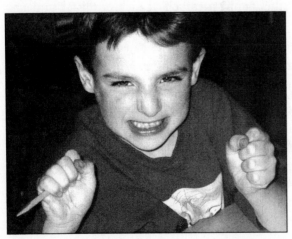 

Sharing a Terrible, Horrible, No Good, Very Bad Day and a Wonderful Day for Alexander

The Polar Express
by Chris Van Allsburg

The train was filled with other children, all in their pajamas and nightgowns. We sang Christmas carols and ate candies with nougat centers as white as snow. We drank hot cocoa as thick and rich as melted chocolate bars. Outside, the lights of towns and villages flickered in the distance as the Polar Express raced northward.

— From *The Polar Express,* page 9

First graders cannot help but envy the children riding on this train. To be drinking the best hot chocolate ever described and eating candy that melts in their mouths as they travel to the North Pole (to perhaps open the "first gift of Christmas" from Santa) would be a dream come true.

As I finished reading *The Polar Express* one December afternoon, Katie wished aloud, "Wouldn't it be fun if we were all in our pajamas, drinking hot chocolate and listening to you read this story?" It occurred to me that this type of incentive could prove useful in getting students to read at home during the winter months ahead; they would gain additional practice with fluency and expression as they read and reread familiar stories. Time spent reading (silently or with a friend) allows first graders to experiment with rhythm, flow, tone, and inflection. Reading fluency improves comprehension by helping the reader focus on making sense of what the author is communicating and how it is being communicated.

At read-aloud the next day, I held up a poster titled "Polar Express Pajama Party" that I had made and challenged students to collectively read 500 books at home. I displayed a copy of the reproducible and parent letter (see pages 40 and 41) and explained how to write the titles of books they read at home to parents, siblings, or other family members. If each of my 21 students could read 24 books in January, we would meet our goal for a Polar Express Pajama Party.

At the beginning of February, we held Room 4's first Polar Express Pajama Party. My students wore their pajamas under loose-fitting clothes and stowed their fuzzy bunny, pig, and dog slippers in their backpacks. After lunch, we wore our pajamas and slippers for a relaxing afternoon of silent reading and story writing. Then, during read-aloud, we had chocolate milk and cookies and revisited *The Polar Express.* As we lined up to go home that day, Katie suggested, "Next we can dress up like the wild things from *Where the Wild Things Are!*"

Rich Vocabulary

roamed *v.* walked about slowly

paced *v.* walked back and forth with excitement

Song and Dance Man
by Karen Ackerman

LEARNING ABOUT   **Writing A List**

Grandpa was a song and dance man who once danced on the vaudeville stage. When we visit, he tells us about a time before people watched TV, back in the good old days, the song and dance days.

— From *Song and Dance Man*, pages 4–6

> ### Rich Vocabulary
>
> **glances** *v.* looks at quickly

One of the first things many children think about doing on a rainy day, an I-don't-know-what-to-do day, or a none-of-my-friends-can-play day is watching television. Instill some other options in your first graders' minds with this springboard activity based on *Song and Dance Man*.

Share the book for read-aloud, and then talk about how much fun the three children had in the attic with Grandpa putting on a show. Then enlist your students' help in writing a list of things to do that are better than TV. Use *Song and Dance Man* to get started, and then watch as your students' imaginations go wild. (This works particularly well during an indoor recess on a rainy day!)

Writing lists in a group setting gives first graders practice in sound-spelling short phrases while reinforcing conventional spelling of previously learned words. This genre also gives students a break from punctuation and writing complete sentences.

Your indoor recess may become a time of toe tapping, joke telling, and song singing that will carry over to rainy days at home.

Things to Do That Are Better Than TV

* Dance to a favorite song. Pretend you're dancing on a vaudeville stage.
* Play dress up: Try on hats and shoes, vests, and bow ties.
* Put on a show for a friend. Sing a song or act out a favorite story.
* Learn a magic trick from a library book.
* Read a joke book.
* Write and illustrate a story.
* Write a letter to your grandma or grandpa.
* Curl up with a pile of favorite books.
* Give your pet a bath.
* Bake cookies with an adult you love.
* Paint a picture.
* Clean your room! You just might discover that favorite lost toy!
* Look at photo albums to relive favorite memories.

Thunderstorm Survey Questions

Teacher Directions: Duplicate, and cut out a survey question for each student.

On a scale of 1-10, how do you feel during a thunderstorm?

not scared at all   1   2   3   4   5   6   7   8   9   10   really scared

On a scale of 1-10, how do you feel during a thunderstorm?

not scared at all   1   2   3   4   5   6   7   8   9   10   really scared

On a scale of 1-10, how do you feel during a thunderstorm?

not scared at all   1   2   3   4   5   6   7   8   9   10   really scared

On a scale of 1-10, how do you feel during a thunderstorm?

not scared at all   1   2   3   4   5   6   7   8   9   10   really scared

On a scale of 1-10, how do you feel during a thunderstorm?

not scared at all   1   2   3   4   5   6   7   8   9   10   really scared

On a scale of 1-10, how do you feel during a thunderstorm?

not scared at all   1   2   3   4   5   6   7   8   9   10   really scared

Use with *Thunder Cake* by Patricia Polacco.

Name _____ Date _____

Directions: Fill in the missing letters. Then draw a picture of a thunder cake at the bottom of the page.

A Recipe for Patricia Polacco's Grandma's Thunder Cake

Cr__ __m together, one at a t__m__:

1 cup shortening

1 3/4 cup sugar

1 t__ __spoon vanilla

3 eggs, separated

(Blend yolks in. B__ __t wh__t__s until they are stiff, then fold in.)

1 cup cold water

1/3 cup pureed tomat__ __s

Sift together:

2 1/2 cups c__k__ flour

1/2 cup dry cocoa

1 1/2 t__ __spoons b__king soda

1 t__ __spoon salt

Mix dry mixture into cr__ __my mixture. B__k__ in two gr__ __sed and floured 8 1/2 inch round pans at 350 degr__ __s for 35 to 40 minutes. Frost with chocolate butter frosting. Top with strawberries.

Use with *Thunder Cake* by Patricia Polacco.

Name _____ Date _____

The Polar Express Pajama Party

Dear Parents,

    To establish good reading-at-home habits this winter, we are embarking on a reading incentive program inspired by *The Polar Express* by Chris Van Allsburg. When the students have collectively read 500 books, we will hold a Polar Express Pajama Party complete with hot chocolate "as thick and rich as melted chocolate bars"—delicious cookies, fuzzy slippers, and favorite jammies, too!

    Doing the following activities with your child will establish good reading habits and help us with our project:

- Set aside a particular time each day to read with your child. Take turns—read some of the story and then have your child read to you.
- Read for at least 15 minutes each day.
- On the attached recording sheet, write the titles of the book(s) you read each day.
- Send the completed sheet to school with your child. A new sheet will be sent home for you to continue recording the books you share. We will tally the number of books on our Polar Express Pajama Party goal poster.
- When students have collectively read 500 books, I will send a note home about the details of the pajama party.

    Thank you for your help in encouraging good reading habits at home. I hope you enjoy the time spent sharing great books with your child.

       Happy Reading!

       _____

       Your Child's Teacher

Use with *The Polar Express* by Chris Van Allsburg.

Polar Express
Reading Incentive Program

I read these books at home.

1. _____

2. _____

3. _____

4. _____

5. _____

6. _____

7. _____

8. _____

9. _____

10. _____

11. _____

12. _____

13. _____

14. _____

15. _____

Parent's Signature: _____

Use with *The Polar Express* by Chris Van Allsburg.

Chapter 3:
Rocking and Rolling With Words
10 Must-Have Books With a Beat

Chapter Objectives:
* exploring real and nonsense rhyming words
* exploring syllables, punctuation, and synonyms
* using phonetic and structural analysis to classify rhyming words
* practicing speaking and listening skills
* sequencing the main events of a story
* reinforcing general reading skills and strategies
* relating stories to personal experiences
* using conventions of spelling in written work
* increasing vocabulary awareness
* enjoying great books with a beat

What better way to motivate students to want to learn to read than by introducing them to the beat of language in rhyming word texts? The must-have books with a beat in this chapter prove that reading is fun and that words can be full of nonsense but they can also often follow a pattern that helps children crack the reading code. Add rhythm instruments such as drums, tambourines, shakers, and rhythm sticks to your read-aloud, and the text and characters' actions come alive with the rhythm of language.

In my days as an elementary school student, *poetry* was a word that immediately produced groans and yawns from many a young child. But thanks to poets like Jack Prelutsky, Shel Silverstein, J. Patrick Lewis, and Lee Bennett Hopkins, *poetry* is no longer a "boring" word but a word that immediately summons up visions of rocking and rolling with language.

Understanding rhyming words is one of the first skills that builds confidence in early readers while arming them with a valuable decoding skill. The power of being able to read just one word (like *king*) leads to the identification of a whole family of other words (*ring, sing, wing, thing, bring,* and so on). The books in this chapter are guaranteed to make your students ask you to "read it again." As the children work on "reading the beat" as the author intended, word identification skills are being reinforced incidentally with every singsong rereading.

Ride with *17 Kings and 42 Elephants* on their rhyming journey through the wild wet night. Hear the monumental crash in *Noisy Nora,* and invent rhyming lines to go with the story. While you read *Feathers for Lunch*, students raise their own word feathers. Do some syllable counting with *Zin! Zin! Zin! A Violin*. Use *Miss Spider's Tea Party* to set aside independent reading time for students. Let students identify and write about their favorite poems in *A Hippopotamusn't*. Let *Something BIG Has Been Here* be the springboard for myriad activities. Help make the world a better place with *Where the Sidewalk Ends.* Initiate tell-me questions after reading aloud *Good Books, Good Times.* Scramble and then sequence the events in *There Was an Old Lady Who Swallowed a Fly.*

Break out the rhythm sticks and handmade drums to rock 'n' roll with the language in these must-have books with a beat.

10 Must-Have Books With a Beat

17 Kings and 42 Elephants by Margaret Mahy

Noisy Nora by Rosemary Wells

Feathers for Lunch by Lois Ehlert

Zin! Zin! Zin! A Violin by Lloyd Moss

Miss Spider's Tea Party by David Kirk

A Hippopotamusn't by J. Patrick Lewis

Something BIG Has Been Here by Jack Prelutsky

Where the Sidewalk Ends by Shel Silverstein

Good Books, Good Times by Lee Bennett Hopkins

There Was an Old Lady Who Swallowed a Fly by Simms Taback

17 Kings and 42 Elephants
by Margaret Mahy

LEARNING ABOUT Identifying and Spelling Rhyming Words

This must-have book with a beat is a book to be read and rocked to with all young children. Each time I read it, I have a greater admiration for Margaret Mahy's ability to tell a story with wonderful nonsense rhyming words. With just a tweak of real words, she is able to forge a meaning and rhyming text all in one.

In the following mini-lesson, I invite students to explore real and nonsense rhyming words to learn spelling patterns. If *happily* is spelled *h-a-p-p-i-l-y,* for example, then *lappily* must be *l-a-p-p-i-l-y*. Students listen to a rereading of the story, and on the reproducible on page 58, record the real and nonsense rhyming word pairs Margaret Mahy uses to tell her tale. This is how I introduce this mini-lesson in my classroom.

Rich Vocabulary

romping *v.* playing

devoured *v.* eaten, made to disappear

Mrs. L.: I've written the first two pages from *17 Kings and 42 Elephants* by Margaret Mahy. Let's read it together:
Seventeen kings on forty-two elephants
Going on a journey through a wild wet night,

Baggy ears like big umbrellaphants,
Little eyes a-gleaming in the jungle light.
What makes this such a fun story to read over and over again?

Vince: The beat—you can almost hear drums thumping when you read it.

Brooke: I like the words she made up like *umbrellaphants*.

Mrs. L.: Nonsense words make this story fun. What two words does *umbrellaphants* sound like?

Class: *Umbrella* and *elephants*.

Katie: It's raining so the elephants need umbrellas.

Daniel: Their ears are like umbrellas so they're *umbrellaphants*.

Mrs. L.: *Umbrellaphants* is such a clever word. I wonder why Margaret Mahy didn't call them something like *umbrellamellas*.

Grace: That wouldn't have rhymed with *elephants*. She needed the word to rhyme with *elephants* so she made up the word *umbrellaphants*.

Mrs. L.: Right! There are two other words that rhyme in these lines . . .

Peter: *Night* and *light*.

Mrs. L.: These rhyming word pairs—real and nonsense—are what give the story a great beat. I have a sheet for you to record the nonsense words and the real words that rhyme in *17 Kings and 42 Elephants*. I'll reread it and stop after each page for you to record the rhyming word pairs. *(I pass out copies of the reproducible on page 58. Then I read a page of the book and stop.)*

> *Seventeen kings saw white-toothed crocodiles*
> *Romping in the river where the reeds grow tall,*
> *Green-eyed dragons, rough as rockodiles,*
> *Lying in the mud where the small crabs crawl.*

William: *Rockodiles* is the nonsense word. It rhymes with *crocodiles*.

Mrs. L.: I wonder why Margaret Mahy invented *rock-o-diles* not *clock-o-diles*?

Maddie: Because the crocodiles are as rough as rocks, not clocks.

Mrs. L.: Margaret Mahy sure invents clever words, doesn't she? I'll write *crocodiles* in book-spelling on the board. Use this word to help you spell *rockodiles* the way Margaret Mahy invented it in the book.

Class: *R-o-c-o-d-i-l-e-s*.

Mrs. L.: Great! You spelled the word as if it were a look-alike rhyming word pair. If you add a *k* to *rock*, you've spelled it the way Margaret Mahy did in her book. How did she spell it?

Class: *R-o-c-k-o-d-i-l-e-s*.

Mrs. L.: Right. What other real rhyming words did you hear on this page? *(I reread the page.)*

Class: *Tall* and *crawl*.

Mrs. L.: Great listening. I'll write *tall* on the board. You spell *crawl* on your sheet.

Josh: *C-r-a-l-l* doesn't look right.

Mrs. L.: Your mind is telling you that the book-spelling for *crawl* is different.

Josh: Yes, but I don't remember what it looked like in the book.

Mrs. L.:	Change the first *l* to a *w* for book-spelling.
Class:	*C-r-a-w-l.*
Mrs. L.:	Nice spelling. Let me read the next two pages.
	Forty-two elephants-oh what a lot of 'ums,
	Big feet beating in the wet wood shade,
	Proud and ponderous hippopotomums
	Danced to the music that the marchers made.
Sara:	*Lot of 'ums* rhymes with *hippopotomums*.
Mrs. L.:	I'm impressed that you remembered "lot of 'ums"! To make *hippos* rhyme with *lot of 'ums*, Margaret Mahy invented or changed *hippopotomus* to *hippopotomum*, and then she added an *s* to show more than one. Let's spell this one together—it's a real challenge. When I spell a word like this, I break the word into smaller chunks and sound it out: *hippo-*, then *–poto-*, and finally *-mums*. I'll write "lot of 'ums" on the board. Now let's spell *hippo-poto-mums*.
Joey:	*Hippo* is *h-i-p-o*.
Grace:	No, it has two *p's—h-i-p-p-o*.
Mrs. L.:	Now try *poto*.
Sara:	*Pot* with an *o. P-o-t-o*.
Mrs. L.:	Great. *Mums* is all that's left to spell.
Brooke:	Add an *m* to lot of *ums* and it's *m-u-m-s*.
Mrs. L.:	Let's put it all together.
Class:	*H-i-p-p-o-p-o-t-o-m-u-m-s*.
Mrs. L.:	That wasn't so bad, was it?
Travis:	No, but it's a thirteen-letter word!
Mrs. L.:	Once you've spelled *hippopotomums*, you can spell anything! What if you wanted to spell *hippopotomus*?
William:	You'd just take away the last *s* and change the last *m* to an *s*.
Mrs. L.:	Excellent! Listen to the next two pages.
	Seventeen kings sang loud and happily,
	Forty-two elephants swayed to the song.
	Tigers at the riverside drinking lappily,
	Knew the kings were happy as they marched along.
Madeline:	*Along* and *song* are the real rhyming words.
Mrs. L.:	Great! Spell *song*.
Class:	*S-o-n-g*.
Mrs. L.:	Great. Now spell *along*.
Class:	*A-l-o-n-g*.
Mrs. L.:	Great spelling. What are the nonsense word pairs?
Jeannie:	Well, *happily* isn't nonsense but it rhymes with the other word—
Jacob:	*Lappily* is nonsense.
Mrs. L.:	What a clever word to describe how the tigers drank water at the riverside.
Emily:	I like how the kings are singing and the elephants are swaying back and forth.

Mrs. L.:	You almost feel like they're moving happily across the page of the book, don't you? Let's spell *happily*.
Class:	*H-a-p-p-i-l-y.*
Mrs. L.:	Right. *Lappily* is a look-alike rhyming word so it's spelled . . .
Class:	*L-a-p-p-i-l-y.*
Mrs. L.:	Great! The next few pages describe the other animals that join the "boom-ba-ba-boom-ba" song. Let's read more.

We continue reading and recording the real and nonsense words. When we finish, our list of rhyming word pairs has helped us gain an understanding of spelling patterns and word families. Perhaps most importantly of all, Margaret Mahy's amazing use of language has proven how full of rhythm our language can be and how this rhythm makes books fun to read—boom-ba-ba-boom-ba, boom-ba-ba-boom-ba.

MORE FUN WITH THE BOOK

Vowel Sounds: As we discuss the tinkling tunesters and twangling trillicans, as well as the ding dong bellicans, the baboonsters and the gorillican, we pull the real word parts from the nonsense parts. When we read "bibble-bubble-babbled to the bing-bang bong," our lesson takes another turn as we explore how one different vowel sound changes the entire word.

Vocabulary: We have a mini-vocabulary lesson as we check the dictionary for *crimson, crystalline,* and *mistalline* to discover that all but *mistalline* are real words.

Moving to the beat of *17 Kings and 42 Elephants*

More Must-Have Books With a Beat

....

Noisy Nora
by Rosemary Wells

LEARNING ABOUT   ## Creating Rhyming Word Pairs

Jack had dinner early, Father read with Kate. Jack needed burping,
so Nora had to wait. First she banged the window. Then she banged
the window, then she dropped her sister's marbles on the kitchen floor.
"Quiet!" said her father. "Hush!" said her mum. "Nora!" said her sister.
"Why are you so dumb?"
— From *Noisy Nora*, pages 7–15

Noisy Nora is a comical and accurate portrayal of sibling rivalry. After a few more attention-getting attempts, Nora does what many young children feel like doing when they're angry with their parents and jealous of attention to a sibling—she runs away. Much to her family's joy, she returns at the end with a "monumental crash."

The content, beat, predictability, and rhyming words make this book a great pick for beginning readers. After reading aloud the story, gather students for another noisy day for Nora. Together, invent other rhyming lines to go along with the predictable pattern and beat of the original text. Use the beginnings of the original lines and then think of what else Nora might do to get the attention of her family. Here are a few of our favorite rewritings.

Another Noisy Nora Day of Rhymes
Father played with Kate so Nora broke a plate.
She slammed the door and then emptied her drawer.
"Hush," said her mum. "Nora," said her sister, "Look at all those crumbs!"
Mother cooked with Kate so Nora threw a skate.
Then she took the baby's bear and threw it down the stairs.
Father read with Kate so Nora ate choco-late.

Rich Vocabulary

moaned *v.* said sadly

As an alternate activity, supply the rhyming words but cover them with sticky notes. For instance, in the first sentence, I would cover the word *plate*. Then let students guess what the words are.

Feathers for Lunch
by Lois Ehlert

 **LEARNING ABOUT** ## Classifying Rhyming Words

Uh-oh. Door's left open, just a crack.
My cat is out and he won't come back!
He's looking for lunch, something new,
a spicy treat for today's menu.
— From *Feathers for Lunch*, pages 5–10

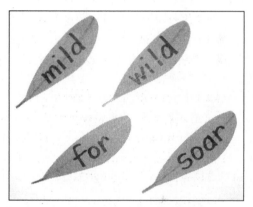

This poor cat, hoping to munch something new and exciting, only catches feathers for lunch. After reading *Feathers for Lunch*, reinforce rhyming word pairs in the context of choral rereadings. Copy individual words from the story onto paper feather cutouts as shown above.

Prior to rereading, distribute the feathers to students. As you reread the story, have them listen for the words written on their feathers. When a student hears the word, he or she can place the feather in a pocket chart. Following the story, sort the feathers into rhyming word pairs. Then identify which pairs are look-alike rhyming word pairs (*mild, wild*) and which are sound-alike rhyming word pairs (*soar, for*) and make a list of them.

For some independent practice, invite pairs of students to listen to *Feathers for Lunch* at the listening center and work together to place the rhyming word feathers in order as the story unfolds.

ON ANOTHER DAY

Have students make their own cat costumes by attaching felt ears to paper headbands and taping on a felt tail. Memorize the story with repeated choral rereadings. Then put on a performance of *Feathers for Lunch* for another class or parents or to videotape.

Rich Vocabulary

snooping *v.* being nosy; looking for

Zin! Zin! Zin! A Violin

by Lloyd Moss

LEARNING ABOUT **Identifying Syllables**

And soaring high and moving in,
With ZIN! ZIN! ZIN! a VIOLIN,
Stroking strings that come alive;
Now QUINTET. Let's count them: FIVE.
— From *Zin! Zin! Zin! A Violin*, page 14

Children can feel the beat of language and read words that make flowing music in *Zin! Zin! Zin! A Violin*. This Caldecott Honor book written by Lloyd Moss and illustrated by Marjorie Priceman will have students identifying and counting syllables, differentiating between a solo and a chamber group of ten, identifying orchestra instruments, and possibly begging to join the band!

Encourage choral readings of the text by asking students to chime in with the capitalized words in the text (see the sample passage above). Next, pass out rhythm sticks so they can make a little music of their own by counting the syllables in the lines of *Zin! Zin! Zin! A Violin*. Reread each page line by line, inviting students to "be your echo" and tap the beats.

READ:	WITH MOURN-FUL MOAN AND SIL-KEN TONE,
TAPS:	1 2 3 4 5 6 7 8

READ:	IT-SELF A-LONE COMES ONE TROM-BONE
TAPS:	1 2 3 4 5 6 7 8

READ:	GLID-ING, SLID-ING, HIGH NOTES GO LOW;
TAPS:	1 2 3 4 5 6 7 8

READ:	ONE TROM-BONE IS PLAY-ING SO-LO.
TAPS:	1 2 3 4 5 6 7 8

Rich Vocabulary

slender *adj.* thin

adore *v.* to love

Although this example illustrates eight beats per line, other pages will provide different numbers of beats for counting and discussing. After trying a few pages together, copy a page on the board and invite individual volunteers to draw lines to break apart each word into smaller chunks or syllables while the rest of the class taps the beats with rhythm sticks. Discuss how dividing words into syllables helps with spelling and sounding out unknown words in reading and writing. Be sure to end the lesson with a final rereading of the book to "put the story back together."

Miss Spider's Tea Party
by David Kirk

 **LEARNING ABOUT**

Reading With Fluency

ONE lonely spider sipped her tea
While gazing at the sky.
She watched the insects on the leaves
And many flying by.
"If I had friends like these," she sighed,
"Who'd stay a while with me.
I'd sit them down on silken chairs
And serve them cakes and tea."
— From *Miss Spider's Tea Party*, page 3

Miss Spider wishes to invite friends to tea. Unfortunately, her invitations go out to insects who fear her spideryness. Miss Spider's table doesn't fill up with guests until one little moth sees her genuinely kind nature and spreads the word to the rest of the insect world. Set up a tea party center where pairs of students can visit with Miss Spider and a few other great books to practice reading with fluency.

Designate an area for Miss Spider's tea party. Provide a child-sized tea set or paper cups, plates and napkins, juice, and shortbread. Include a basket of books for pairs of students to read together. *Miss Spider's Tea Party* and the rest of the Miss Spider series are sure picks for this tea party book basket. Don't forget to include the board book version of *Miss Spider's Tea Party—The Counting Book.* This shortened version is great for beginning readers to read independently.

Rich Vocabulary

courtesy *n.* a polite act or gesture

fragile *adj.* easily broken, delicate

Each day, during silent reading time, invite two students to "tea." As children peruse books and enjoy a snack together, they brush up on their reading skills and manners with Miss Spider and her other book friends.

A Hippopotamusn't
by J. Patrick Lewis

Writing About a Favorite Poem

A hippopotamusn't sit
On lawn chairs, stools, and rockers.
A hippopotamusn't yawn
   Directly under tightrope walkers.
A hippopotamusn't roll
   In gutters used by bowlers.
A hippopotamusn't fail
To floss his hippopotamolars.
The awful things a hippopotamusn't do
Are just
As important as the lawful things
A hippopotamust.
   — Title poem from *A Hippopotamusn't,* page 39

J. Patrick Lewis's *A Hippopotamusn't* is filled with clever word play verses with an animal theme. "Informational" poems such as "Rules for the Elephant Parade," "The Culture of the Vulture," "How the Rhinoceros Got His Nose," and "How to Trick a Chicken" keep students listening for the punch line. You'll find yourself reading these zany poems again and again upon request.

Students will enjoy talking about this collection of poems—from the clever words like *hippopotamolars,* and *fellow-phant* to the shape poem of the flamingo and the word plays in "Tom Tigercat" who "wouldn't think of lion, no, he doesn't cheetah bit." As students discuss the poems, they're exploring vocabulary and expanding their literary language, sharpening listening and speaking skills (as well as following the rules of conversation!), and relating the poems to their own experiences.

Hold a poetry celebration where everyone selects a favorite poem from *A Hippopotamusn't* and writes a few sentences revealing why the poem is a favorite. Students can share their ideas and then recite their favorite J. Patrick Lewis poems.

Rich Vocabulary

ridiculous *adj.* very funny

Something BIG Has Been Here

by Jack Prelutsky

Vocabulary, Spelling, Synonyms, Punctuation

Something big has been here,
what it was, I do not know,
for I did not see it coming,
and I did not see it go,
but I hope I never meet it,
if I do, I'm in a fix,
for it left behind its footprints,
they are size nine-fifty-six.

— From *Something BIG Has Been Here,* page 7

The quote on the back cover of *Something BIG Has Been Here* begins, "If you are twelve or under, you have probably read—and memorized at least one poem by Jack Prelutsky." I would add this to the quote: "If you are a teacher of first-grade children, you have probably read—and memorized at least one Jack Prelutsky book!" And if you haven't, it's great summer reading material—and you'll find yourself armed with hundreds of quick, attention-grabbing segues into lessons of all kinds. Here are ten of my favorite poems and activities for enjoying this book with my students.

Some BIG Ideas from *Something BIG Has Been Here*

1. **"The Zoo Was in an Uproar":** Teach a lesson on synonyms in which the animals complain of how repellant, disgusting, appalling, disgraceful and barbaric it was on the day the hippopotamus forgot to take a bath.

2. **"Squirrels":** This poem is great for introducing question marks since they're the shape of squirrels' tails.

3. **"Happy Birthday, Mother Dearest":** Copy this poem to use as a cloze activity where students fill it in to make a birthday card for Mom.

4. **"The Turkey Shot out of the Oven":** Have students learn this fun Thanksgiving poem.

5. **"Something Big Has Been Here":** Use this poem to introduce a dinosaur unit.

6. **"My Fish Can Ride a Bicycle":** Create a new fill-in-the-blank poem following this simple pattern.

> ## Rich Vocabulary
>
> **uproar** *n.* lots of excitement
>
> **chuckled** *v.* laughed

7. **"As Soon as Fred Gets out of Bed"**: Just plain silly, this favorite of first graders covers different learning goals with each reading: Count the syllables in each line; add *deftly* and *croons* to students' rich vocabulary; use the theme of underwear as a springboard to a memorable lesson on compound words.

8. **"Grasshopper Gumbo"**: Students are quick to memorize this poem due to its fun beat and the volume of requested rereading.

9. **"My Snake"**: Gain some alphabet, handwriting, and vocabulary practice with this snake who's learning the alphabet.

10. **"I Want a Pet Porcupine, Mother"**: This poem is perfect for quotation mark practice.

Whatever the learning goal, Jack Prelutsky is sure to lend a hand with the multitude of motivating, rhyming stories in this collection of sure-to-be favorites.

....

Where the Sidewalk Ends
by Shel Silverstein

LEARNING ABOUT

Building Social Studies Vocabulary

On Friday afternoons, at the end of each school year, our primary division of first and second graders holds "related activities." Students from each of our five classrooms are mixed together to form five new related activity groups, which allows everyone time to get to know students and teachers from other classes. These groups rotate to each of the five primary teachers for a 30-minute unit-based activity. As they rotate to the different classrooms, students might work on an art activity, learn a song, play a game, or work on a science project.

When students arrive in my classroom, I read aloud a great book. One year, using Shel Silverstein's *Where the Sidewalk Ends,* I highlighted a few favorite poems around the theme of "Making the World a Better Place." We read "Hug O' War" to discuss the prospects of a world where everyone hugs, giggles, kisses, grins, cuddles, and wins. We agreed that it really makes "No Difference" if we were small, big, rich, poor, red, black, orange, yellow, or white since we're all the same when we turn off the lights. We end our related activities with a visit to "Hector the Collector" to brainstorm ideas for recycling his treasure trunk items into something more than junk.

To extend the activity in your classroom, provide poster paper, crayons, markers, and paint so students can illustrate a "Making the World a Better Place" poster using ideas from one of Shel Silverstein's poems.

Rich Vocabulary

collection *n.* a group of things put together

collector *n.* one who gathers certain things

Good Books, Good Times!
by Lee Bennett Hopkins

LEARNING ABOUT   **Relating Personal Experiences To Poems**

Give me a book
and long tall grass,
There will I look
as the hours pass . . .
— From "Give Me a Book" by Myra Cohn Livingston, page 13

The first few lines of this poem by Myra Cohn Livingston tell it like it is for book-lovers. And poet David McCord describes getting hooked on books like this: "Books fall open, you fall in, delighted where you've never been . . ."

In this book of poems about the joy of reading, Lee Bennett Hopkins has selected works by some of the best children's poets of our time to inspire young children to put reading at the top of their list of entertainment. Use this collection of poems to get students into the habit of reading at home every night. Read aloud the title poem "Good Books, Good Times!" and then follow up with tell-me questions to stimulate a good books discussion and help students make personal connections to poetry. Here are some samples from my classroom.

Tell Me About:

- a place where you've been known to read books (a closet, a tent, under a table, and so on)
- a world you've entered in a book
- a book that has made you think of someone or something you might want to become
- a time you got lost in a book and maybe almost missed dinner
- a book you just had to keep reading
- a book you'd recommend to classmates for summer reading
- a "what-if" about a book ("What if you opened a book about dinosaurs and one stumbled out?")
- something amazing you "did" in a book (found a pot of gold, wrestled with a troll, met a dragon face to face?)
- a make-believe book you've read and reread
- what kind of story you like best (mystery, dinosaurs, animals, scary)
- how many books you think you've read so far

> ## Rich Vocabulary
>
> **unexpected** *adj.*
> all of a sudden
>
> **vanished** *v.*
> disappeared

MORE FUN WITH THE BOOK

At the beginning of each month, distribute My Calendar of Good Books for Good Times (see sample, next page). Students can record the books they read at home on these calendars.

At the end of the month, they return their calendars and participate in a recommendations session to kick off a new month of more good books for more good times.

Name **Maggie**

In the spaces below, record the titles of books you read at home.

Good Books for Good Times!

My Calendar of Good Books for GoodTimes!

November

Sunday	Monday	Tuesday	Wednesday	Thursday	Friday	Saturday
						1 Arthur's Thanksgiving
2 Noisy Nora	3 Hedgie's Surprise	4 O.W. Thinks Big	5 Mr. Putter and Tabby Pick the Pears	6 Dragon Gets By	7 Comet's Nine Lives	8 Nuts to You
9 Stellaluna	10 Charlie Anderson	11 The Cat in the Hat	12 Silly Tilly's Thanksgiving	13 Benjamin and Tulip	14 Strega Nona	15 The First Thanksgiving
16 Lady and the Tramp	17 Thanksgiving on Thursday	18 A Turkey for Thanksgiving	19 The Perfect Thanksgiving	20 Green Eggs and Ham	21 Fox in Socks	22 A Perfect Thanksgiving
23 Owl Moon / Clifford's Thanksgiving 30	24 Arthur's Thanksgiving	25 Thanksgiving at the Tappletons	26 'Twas the Night Before Thanksgiving	27 Happy Thanksgiving!	28 Silly Tilly's Thanksgiving	29 Night Tree

Parent Signature **K. Sorrell**

My Calendar of Good Books for Good Times!

··

There Was an Old Lady Who Swallowed a Fly
by Simms Taback

LEARNING ABOUT

Sequencing Events

When it comes to retelling this folk poem first heard in the United States in the 1940s, there's no beating Simms Taback's version. As the hole in the old lady's stomach grows to accommodate the increasing size of her meals, so does children's enthusiasm for this great book. The colorful collage details are filled with items for students to pore over, including a newspaper clipping for the "Cat in Hat Loses Hat," a recipe for Spider Soup, a Lost Dog poster, and a cover from *Time* magazine featuring an article titled "Senior Swallows Cat."

Add a little fun to the endless requests for rereading by having students make their own Old Lady mini-books.

Rich Vocabulary

gulped *v.* swallowed quickly

devoured *v.* made to disappear, eaten

Teaching With Favorite Read-Alouds in First Grade

Pages of The Old Lady Who Swallowed a Fly mini-book

Step 1: Make a cardboard template of the Old Lady. (Be sure to make her big enough to accommodate each of the six animals she eats).

Step 2 (book cover): Trace the template onto a sheet of white paper. Leave space at the top for the book title. (You may also let students trace the template directly onto a sheet of colored paper or construction paper.) Duplicate a copy for each student, and have him or her color the old lady and complete the page.

Step 3 (page 1): Trace the Old Lady template on another sheet of white paper. Draw six concentric circles, one for each animal, about 1/2 inch apart in the center of the Old Lady. At the top of this page, write the following: There was an old lady who swallowed a ____. Duplicate a copy for each student, and instruct him or her to color and complete this page.

Step 4 (page 2): After students decide which animal to portray, help them cut out the appropriate circle on the page 1 Old Lady. For instance, cut out the largest circle to show the cow, the smallest to show the fly, and so on. Then tell students to draw the animal that will fit inside the hole on a separate sheet of paper. (They can trace the cutout circle on page 1 on this sheet of paper and then draw the animal inside it.) Attach page 2 behind page 1 so the animal is visible in the Old Lady's stomach.

Step 5 (page 3): Duplicate and distribute copies of page 59 to students. Ask them to cut out the strips. Then they should arrange the strips in the correct order and glue them on a sheet of white paper.

Step 6 (back cover): Give each student a sheet of paper to serve as the back cover. After placing the pages of their mini-books in order, they can staple the spines.

After rereading the story, display the mini-books in your classroom.

Teaching With Favorite Read-Alouds in First Grade

Rhyme Time

Directions: Write the rhyming word pairs from the story on the lines below.

Nonsense Rhyming Word Pairs	Real Rhyming Word Pairs
elephants	night
umbrellaphants	light
crocodiles	tall
_____	_____
lot of 'ums	shade
_____	_____
happily	song
_____	_____
pelicans	fantails
_____	_____
trillicans	trees
_____	_____

Write the remaining real and nonsense rhyming word pairs on the back.

Use with *17 Kings and 42 Elephants* by Margaret Mahy.

Teaching With Favorite Read-Alouds in First Grade

Name _____ Date _____

What the Old Lady Ate

Directions: Cut out the lines from *There Was an Old Lady*.
Paste them in the correct order.

She swallowed the bird to catch the spider.

She swallowed the dog to catch the cat.

She swallowed the spider to catch the fly.

She swallowed the cow to catch the dog.

She swallowed the cat to catch the bird.

I don't know why she swallowed the fly.

Perhaps she'll die.

Use with *There Was an Old Lady Who Swallowed a Fly* by Simms Taback.

Chapter 4:
How Much? How Long? How Many?
10 Must-Have Books for Teaching Math and Science

Chapter Objectives:

* ✳ representing numbers from 50 to 100 with objects
* ✳ exploring ordinal number words
* ✳ estimating, counting, and comparing
* ✳ making and interpreting picture and bar graphs
* ✳ ordering different-sized containers
* ✳ working with a calendar to understand measurements of time
* ✳ working cooperatively to improve our environment
* ✳ increasing vocabulary awareness
* ✳ enriching the learning of math and science concepts with great read-alouds

Fortunately, for first graders who by nature have limited attention spans, math manipulatives and hands-on science lessons can make them active participants in the learning process. Introduce a few great books to the math and science mix, and a new dimension in attention is added.

Relate learning about patterns to *Knots on a Counting Rope* by Bill Martin Jr. and John Archambault. How much is a million? Read David Schwartz's book and find out. Invite Ed Young's *Seven Blind Mice* to a lesson on addition, sorting, and ordinal number practice. Are you teaching estimation and counting? Estimate and count coins to fill jars just like the family did in *A Chair for My Mother* by Vera B. Williams. Let *The Bookshop Dog* and *The Grouchy Ladybug* make lessons on telling time, graphing, and ordering objects by size more appealing.

When it comes to hands-on-science lessons, introduce plants and seeds with *Tops and Bottoms,* and then have students plant some tops and bottoms for themselves. *Stellaluna* and *Frog and Toad Are Friends* can take learning about animals to a higher level, while *Miss Rumphius* will inspire an Earth Day science lesson.

The must-have books in this chapter for teaching math and science keep motivation and relevance to the real world a top priority for concepts such as subtraction, estimation, graphing, problem solving, plants, and animals.

---

10 Must-Have Books for Teaching Math and Science

Knots on a Counting Rope by Bill Martin Jr. and John Archambault

How Much Is a Million? by David M. Schwartz

Seven Blind Mice by Ed Young

A Chair for My Mother by Vera B. Williams

The Bookshop Dog by Cynthia Rylant

The Grouchy Ladybug by Eric Carle

Tops and Bottoms by Janet Stevens

Frog and Toad Are Friends by Arnold Lobel

Stellaluna by Janell Cannon

Miss Rumphius by Barbara Cooney

Knots on a Counting Rope

by Bill Martin Jr. & John Archambault

LEARNING ABOUT Identifying Patterns

Now, Boy . . .
now that the story has been told again,
I will tie another knot
on the counting rope.
When the rope is filled with knots,
you will know the story by heart
and can tell it to yourself.

— From *Knots on a Counting Rope,* page 30

The illustration accompanying the text above shows Grandfather adding another knot to a counting rope that is nearly filled. Soon, Boy will know the story by heart. To help my first graders identify and repeat a few patterns by heart, I reread *Knots on a Counting Rope.* Together we keep track of all the little stories inside the big story by adding a large colorful bead to a string. Our class counting and pattern rope is a favorite math lesson that gives students a hands-on way to explore patterns, a fundamental math concept for primary-age children.

To prepare for this lesson, I gather one long length of string and several large wooden beads in assorted colors. I also cut a length of string for each student and tie a knot at one end. I place smaller beads into several paper cups for them to share at seatwork areas.

This math lesson on patterns and counting also turns into a literary discussion about overcoming adversity, accepting individual differences, and descriptive language.

Rich Vocabulary

frail *adj.* weak

courage *n.* strong, brave

Mrs. L.:	Do you remember what the counting rope was used for in *Knots on a Counting Rope* by Bill Martin Jr. and John Archambault?
Maddie:	Every time they told the story about the boy, the grandfather tied another knot on the counting rope.
Mrs. L.:	Right. Grandfather said, "When the rope is filled with knots . . ."
Maddie :	The boy would know the story by heart.
Mrs. L.:	Right again. There were lots of little stories inside the big story. I thought it would be fun for us to make a counting rope of our own. Instead of tying a knot, I'll add a bead for each of the little stories you remember from *Knots on a Counting Rope*. The beads will be easier for you to see. Along with counting, we'll make a pattern with the beads. Tell me about a little story inside the big story.
Billy:	There was the story of how the boy was born on a stormy night.
Mrs. L.:	I'll add a red bead for your first idea.
Katie:	The grandfather had to go and get the grandmother, and he was afraid.
Mrs. L.:	"Heart-pounding afraid," the book says. I'll add a blue bead for that story.
Greg:	How about the part where the blue horses gave the boy strength to live?
Emily:	I like how when the boy was a baby, he held out his arms to the horses.
Jacob:	He was grabbing their strength. You should add another blue bead for the blue horses.
Mrs. L.:	Good idea. So far we have red, blue, blue beads for three ideas.
Daniel:	Don't forget the story about the boy being blind. Grandfather called that "crossing the dark mountains."
Jeannie:	It means bad times in our lives.
Mrs. L.:	Or challenges. Do you remember what the grandfather called the boy's blindness?
Joey:	He said, "He was born with a dark sheet in front of his eyes."
Mrs. L.:	I think he called it a dark curtain. I'll add a black bead, a dark one, for his blindness. What else do you remember from the story?
Vince:	The boy named his horse Rainbow because he was born just when a rainbow was in the sky one morning. Use a bright color for that.
Katie:	How about orange for sunrise?
Mrs. L.:	Good idea. Now we have red, blue, blue, black, orange beads on our rope.
Casey:	Add another bead for how Rainbow and Boy practiced riding the trails together.
Peter:	Use green. I picture green when they're riding on the trails.
Mrs. L.:	Sure. We have red, blue, blue, black, orange, green beads.
Sara:	Add a bead for the race that they were in and almost won. Use red—they raced with all their hearts. Red is for hearts.
Mrs. L.:	That's wonderful remembering. Boy raced with all his heart over the dark mountain. I love the words on this page where the grandfather walks with Boy and Rainbow. Look how proud Grandfather is of Boy—you can see his pride in the way he's holding his head high.
Brooke:	Look at the smiling faces of the people watching.

Teaching With Favorite Read-Alouds in First Grade

Bobby:	They just saw a blind boy race on a horse. He could have crashed into anything, but he raced like the wind and didn't crash.
Christy:	And almost won. I wish he had won.
Mrs. L.:	He didn't win the race, but he won much more.
William:	The boy won a race with his blindness, and blindness didn't win.
Travis:	And he didn't crash!
Grace:	And he learned to see with his heart. I like that part. I could listen to this story over and over again.
Mrs. L.:	I could, too. Let's take a look at our counting rope pattern.
Class:	Red, blue, blue, black, orange, green, red.
Maddie:	It starts all over again with red.
Jacob:	We made a pattern!
Mrs. L.:	Yes, we did. Let's continue the pattern. What color bead would come next?
Casey:	Blue, blue.
Greg:	Then black.
Vince:	Orange, green.
Makenzie:	Then it starts all over again.
Mrs. L.:	How many steps are in this pattern?
Class:	Six.
Vince:	But there are only five colors. There are two blues.
Mrs. L.:	Great! Let's see if we can fill the rope with more beads. Make a quick circle, and we'll pass the rope around. When it's your turn, add a bead to continue the pattern. Then, I'll give you a chance to make counting ropes of your own.

We continue to discuss the story while the counting rope is passed around the circle. Next, students return to their seats with the lengths of string and cups of small colored beads to make individual counting ropes with a 5- or 6-step pattern.

At read-aloud that day, we begin a class counting rope for books we've shared. I grab a stack of ten favorite books, and together we add a bead for each book until a 5-step pattern appears. We continue the pattern as each new book is shared. On a chart titled "The Stories We Know by Heart," I record the names of the books using colored markers to represent the corresponding bead on the counting rope. Our counting rope pattern grows throughout the year as we read more great books and learn them by heart.

Our counting ropes

More Must-Have Books for Teaching Math and Science

How Much Is a Million?
by David M. Schwartz

LEARNING ABOUT **Representing Large Numbers**

How much is a million? How big is a billion? How tremendous is a trillion? Well, according to this book written by David M. Schwartz and illustrated by Steven Kellogg, counting to a million would take about 23 days, counting to a billion would take 95 years, and counting to a trillion would take about 200,000 years—without breaks for eating and sleeping! Since we all know how precious time in the classroom is—and the fact that a few parents may object to the lack of meals and sleep—it's probably best to have students count and depict numbers to 100, 200, 300, 400 and 500 or even 1,000 since these numbers can easily be counted during one math period.

How Much Is a Million? is written just the way young mathematicians think—concretely and pictorially. One million children standing on one another's shoulders would reach higher than airplanes can fly; a goldfish bowl big enough for a million goldfish would be large enough to hold a whale. And if you're wondering what 1,000,000 tiny stars would look like, go on the seven-page journey illustrating 100,000 stars ten times, and you'll see a million stars!

Take students on an "arithmetic journey with Marvelosissimo the Mathematical magician." Select a number goal from 100 to 1,000 for students to explore. If your goal is 200, for example, have students find a container that can hold 200

If 2oo Teddy Bear counters were placed shoulder to shoulder, they would reach across the classroom.

Unifix cubes, line up 200 Teddy Bear counters, measure something that is 200 inches, or think of things they can do in 200 seconds. Use a camera to capture these numbers pictorially and then make them into a book called *How Much Is 200?* Each of my students included 200 pictures—stars, balloons, or smiley faces—for a page in their book.

Rich Vocabulary

estimate *v.* to make a careful guess based on what you know

Seven Blind Mice

by Ed Young

LEARNING ABOUT Addition Facts And Number Stories

The Mouse Moral: Knowing in part may make a fine tale,
but wisdom comes from seeing the whole.
— From *Seven Blind* Mice, page 39

Each time I read this book, I think of a new lesson to teach. The simple, short, and enjoyable text spawns rereadings and applications to many lessons. During the first read-aloud of *Seven Blind Mice* to my class, I ask my students what it would be like to be blind and "see" the strange Something for the first time. Immediately, they identify the Something as an elephant, but they can also understand how the different parts of the elephant are regarded by each of the mice: "leg is a red pillar to red mouse, trunk is a green snake to green mouse, tusk is a yellow spear to yellow mouse, head is a great cliff to purple mouse, ear is an orange fan to orange mouse, tail is a blue rope to blue mouse." But the white mouse takes the whole animal into account and discovers that it's an elephant.

I turn the mouse moral of parts to whole into a mouse math lesson on sums to seven using the Seven Blind Mice cutouts on reproducible page 74 and the Story Mat reproducible on page 75. Invent Seven Blind Mice number stories such as the ones below, and then have small groups of students use the mouse cutouts to find sums to seven.

> ## Rich Vocabulary
>
> **wisdom** *n.* having an understanding of something

Seven Blind Mice Math

- Red Mouse, Orange Mouse, and Green Mouse are swinging on Something's tail. Purple Mouse and Red Mouse join in. How many mice in all are swinging on Something's tail?
- White Mouse and Red Mouse are on Something's right ear. Blue Mouse and Purple Mouse are on Something's left ear. Red Mouse and Orange Mouse are on its back. How many mice are on Something altogether?
- The mice are using Something's trunk as a slide into the pond. Red Mouse and Purple Mouse slide down together. Green Mouse, White Mouse, Blue Mouse, and Orange Mouse wait their turns on a tusk. Write a number sentence to describe these slide antics.

Set up a center where students can invent their own number stories for friends to solve. Have them use felt mice cutouts on a flannel board with the strange Something as a background.

ON ANOTHER DAY

When teaching ordinal numbers, I invite the seven blind mice to our lesson and introduce seven felt mice in different colors (red, green, yellow, purple, orange, blue, and white). I arrange the seven mice in mixed order on the flannel board and use a permanent marker to write the ordinal number words *first* through *seventh* onto white flannel strips and place these in mixed order on the flannel board, too. As I reread the story, students help me place the mice in appropriate order from first through seventh with the corresponding ordinal number words underneath.

Seven Blind Mice Flannel Board Center

After discussing the mouse moral and its implications to other situations, I bring the book to a writers' workshop lesson on analogies. (See *Literature Based Mini-Lessons to Teach Writing* by Susan Lunsford, Scholastic Professional Books, 1998.)

> ## TEACHING TIP
>
> Use these flannel mice to reinforce color words. Make flannel labels for each of the colors, and have students match the color word with the appropriate mouse.

A Chair for My Mother
by Vera B. Williams

LEARNING ABOUT Estimating, Counting, And Comparing

"There's no good place for me to take a load off my feet," she says. When Grandma wants to sit back and hum and cut up potatoes, she has to get as comfortable as she can on a hard kitchen chair.

So that is how come Mama brought home the biggest jar she could find at the diner and all the coins started to go into the jar.

— From *A Chair for My Mother*, page 21

After their house and all their belongings burn in a fire, a family is forced to save their coins to buy a new chair—not just any chair but "A wonderful, beautiful, fat, soft armchair . . . one covered in velvet with roses all over it . . . the best chair in the whole world." Each evening, Mother's tips from the Blue Tile Diner, Grandma's spare grocery change, and the narrator's money from filling the ketchup bottles at the diner go into their saving jar. When the jar is filled, they'll have enough to buy their dream chair.

Use this heartwarming story of saving and working together to help your students estimate and count coins. Divide the class into groups of four, and supply each group with a small mayonnaise or pickle jar. Give each group objects such as marbles, pennies, paper clips, erasers, large pasta shapes, and other assorted items. Have students estimate how many of a particular object it will take to fill the jar. After counting the actual number of objects, let students choose another object to fill the same jar. After estimating, filling the jar, and counting several different objects, distribute smaller or larger jars to groups so they can estimate and fill them for more size and shape comparisons.

MORE FUN WITH THE BOOK

Think about raising funds for a first-grade project. One year, the students in each of our three first-grade classrooms participated in an Adopt a Whale project. A letter was sent home asking parents to help students "earn" ten cents to donate to the cause. After each class raised money, we sent a check for the amount saved and anxiously waited for our news of our whale. Within a few weeks, we received a photograph of our whale with information about her. Students made adoption announcements informing family and friends of the happy event.

The Bookshop Dog
by Cynthia Rylant

LEARNING ABOUT  **Picture and Bar Graphs**

Once there was a woman who loved her dog so much that she could hardly bear to be away from her . . .
— From *The Bookshop Dog*, page 3

As the owner of two spoiled Labrador retrievers, I can understand where Cynthia Rylant's inspiration came from for this book. Her photograph on the book with the real Martha Jane shows how strong the bond between them is. After sharing this story with my class, I can't resist telling a few tails—I means tales—about my two Labs, Sydney and Jordan.

To give students an opportunity to talk about their own pets and to compare the pets of fellow classmates, we make picture and bar graphs. During our study of graphs, a question is posted when students arrive in the morning. Depending on the type of graph, they are asked to add a Unifix cube, attach a sticky note or sticker, or tape a small dog bone as a way of providing data for each graph of the day. I kick off math lessons by discussing and interpreting the results of the graph that day. Here are some of the questions I've used in my classroom.

Our Five Favorite Questions for
***The Bookshop Dog*-Based Graphs**

1. Where does your pet sleep?

   in a pet bed   in a family member's bed

   in a crate   in his/her own special place

2. What would Martha Jane like for her birthday?

   beefy bones   tennis balls

   a new leash and collar   a surfboard

3. What do you think Martha Jane's favorite bedtime story is?

   Henry and Mudge in Puddle Trouble by Cynthia Rylant

   Cat Kong by Dav Pilkey

   Dogzilla by Dav Pilkey

   Dog Heaven by Cynthia Rylant

   The Cookie Store Cat by Cynthia Rylant

4. Next to beefy bones, what is Martha Jane's favorite dog treat?

   Dog Yums   Wag Snacks

   Dog Chews   "Frosty Paws" Ice Cream

5. Who would be Martha Jane's second-best choice for a dog-sitter?

   policeman   band director

   postman   children

To offer students an opportunity to choose a book for read-aloud, I display a graph entitled "What Should We Read Today?" next to our gathering space. Prior to read-aloud, the children offer input by attaching a Unifix Cube next to their book choice. After quickly tallying the results of the graph, we settle in for Martha Jane's Book Club pick-of-the-day.

Martha Jane's Book Club:
What Should We Read Today?

The Grouchy Ladybug
by Eric Carle

Investigating Size and Shapes

Eric Carle's grouchy ladybug first picked a fight with a fellow ladybug, then a yellow jacket, a stag beetle, a praying mantis, and a sparrow—all the way up to a whale—before learning to pick on somebody its own size. Let students explore the concept of size and shape at a learning center book-based activity.

Gather plastic containers of different sizes and shapes such as yogurt containers, ice cream buckets, ketchup bottles, and so on, and invite students to order them from smallest to largest. Provide rice or water and a dumping area where students can experiment to see which container holds more; for example, they'll rationalize that "More fits in this container so it must be bigger."

MORE FUN WITH THE BOOK

1. Write the names of animals with gradually larger letters to match the size of the animal. (Look at the book for an example).
2. Have a manners lesson using a grouchy ladybug glove puppet and a few other well-behaved, more humble puppets.
3. Practice telling time to the hour and quarter hour.
4. Make a collage cutout of the grouchy ladybug with symmetrical spots.
5. Observe real ladybugs in the spring—or research them at the library or on the Internet.

Rich Vocabulary

suggested *v.* gave an idea

insist *v.* to ask strongly

Other Must-Have Books by Eric Carle

The Very Clumsy Click Beetle
The Very Hungry Caterpillar
The Very Busy Spider
The Very Lonely Firefly
The Very Noisy Cricket

Tops and Bottoms
by Janet Stevens

LEARNING ABOUT
Growing Vegetables

What do you get when you cross a Clever Hare with a Lazy Bear?

A. a lesson on the virtues of working hard

B. a science lesson on growing plants

C. a Caldecott Honor book by Janet Stevens called *Tops and Bottoms*

D. all of the above

The answer, of course, is D. Open the cover of Janet Stevens's book from top to bottom, and pore over each detailed and warmly illustrated two-page spread. Bear's ever-changing sleeping poses, Hare's rambunctious little hares, and the expressions on all the animals' faces make *Tops and Bottoms* a favorite.

This must-have book makes a great book-based science lesson on plants and how they grow. Following a read-aloud, we pause to write the best parts of plants on a chart.

The Best Part of Plants

Tops	Bottoms	Middles
lettuce	carrots	corn
broccoli	radishes	
celery	beets	

Then we grow a few of our own plants. In a windowsill garden, we plant lettuce and corn seeds in soil-filled paper cups. We place toothpicks in carrot stems, put them in water-filled cups until their roots grow, and then plant them. Hardworking hares see how diligence pays off, while lazy bears learn an important lesson—although they hardly do any work.

Rich Vocabulary

clever *adj.* smart

scowl *v.* to frown

Frog and Toad Are Friends

by Arnold Lobel

LEARNING ABOUT

Measuring Time (Calendars)

Toad went back into the house.
He got into the bed and pulled the covers over his head again.
"But, Toad," cried Frog, "you will miss all the fun!"
"Listen, Frog," said Toad. "How long have I been asleep?"
"You have been asleep since November," said Frog.
"Well then," said Toad, "a little more sleep will not hurt me. Come back
again and wake me up at about half past May. Good night, Frog."

— From *Frog and Toad Are Friends,* pages 10–11

Like Toad, there are times when we'd all like to stay in bed until half past May. And we all need a clever friend like Frog to shake us out of bed. Frog tears the pages from November to April from Toad's calendar so that May is on top. Then he wakes Toad and shows him the calendar. Toad exclaims that is May and climbs out of bed.

This chapter of *Frog and Toad Are Friends* called "Spring" makes for a fun math lesson on seasons, months, and calendar facts. Using a flip-top calendar, talk about the following ideas:

Calendar Fun with Frog and Toad

- What is half past May?
- If Toad's birthday is May 13, would he have slept through his own birthday?
- How many months would Toad have slept from November until May?
- How long did Toad really sleep?
- Frog's birthday was November 12. Toad went to sleep on November 20. How many days was Toad awake after Frog's birthday?
- What season did Toad fall asleep? If he woke up in May, what season was it then? What season did he sleep through?
- Divide the months of the year into seasons.
- List all the months with 30 days and 31 days. Which month is missing?
- Which month has the most birthdays in your class? Which month has the least?
- Mark a few upcoming special events on a calendar. Count the days until these events.

Rich Vocabulary

considerate *adj.*
show kindness to someone

Sorting and Classifying: We read the chapter called "The Lost Button" and then set up a button sorting center where students sort a collection of buttons using attributes such as color, number of holes, size, shape, and thickness. We save any "white, four-holed, big, round, thick buttons" for Toad, just in case he loses another one sometime in the future.

· ·

Stellaluna

by Janell Cannon

Investigating Animals (Bats)

"Is that one of your first graders' favorite books?" my young son, Ryan, asked as he pointed to the copy of *Stellaluna* next to my computer. He didn't wait for an answer but continued, "I really like that book, too. That's why I wanted to be a bat for Halloween. Look at Stellaluna's cute little face. See her little tongue flapping as she flies? She is a friendly bat. Real bats do things to help us, don't they, Mommy? I have an idea. You could take a break from your computer and read it for a 'couple of whiles.'"

Knowing how persistent my son can be once he gets an idea, I put my computer to sleep and read *Stellaluna* to him. Together, we enjoyed the warm illustrations that accompany this tale of a baby bat that becomes separated from her mother and lives with a family of birds. "I love when the Mommy sniffs Stellaluna's fur and knows she's her baby," Ryan commented at the end of the book, "I think this might be my most favorite book. Read it again, please."

Bat finger puppet

My first graders share similar thoughts when we enjoy *Stellaluna* for read-aloud. After several rereadings and requests to borrow my copy for silent reading time, we make Stellaluna finger puppets that double as bookmarks.

For a science lesson on mammals, I use the "Bat Notes" on the last two pages of the book. I rephrase the following true statements, making some of them false as students hold up their bat puppets each time I read a true bat fact.

Rich Vocabulary

startle *v.* to surprise someone

peculiar *adj.* different or odd-looking

Bat Facts

• Bats sleep all day and are awake all night. They are nocturnal.
• Bats have wings attached to their hands.
• The most famous of all bats is the vampire bat.

- Many bats eat insects. Others eat fish, amphibians, and reptiles.
- There are nearly one thousand different kinds of bats.
- Some bats have wingspans of nearly six feet.
- Fruit bats have long muzzles, large eyes, pointy ears, and furry bodies.
- Fruit bats are nicknamed flying foxes.
- Bats are mammals.
- Bats are the only mammals capable of powered flight.
- Fruit bats use their keen senses of vision and smell to help them fly.
- Other bats use echolocation or sound waves to help them travel.

Miss Rumphius
by Barbara Cooney

 **LEARNING ABOUT** **Exploring Conservation**

"When I grow up," I tell her, "I too will go to faraway places and come home to live by the sea."
"That is all very well, little Alice," says my aunt, "but there is a third thing you must do."
"What is that?" I ask.
"You must do something to make the world more beautiful."
"All right," I say.
But I do not know yet what that can be . . .
   —From *Miss Rumphius,* page 9

Miss Rumphius's great-niece doesn't know what she can do to make the world more beautiful. Do your students have any ideas about how they can make their school and grounds more beautiful? Have small groups make plans to do just that. Meet together as a class to brainstorm and finalize a final plan and submit it to the principal for a Clean-Up Day. For instance, will the class pick up trash on the playground or recycle cans and other recyclables at lunch?

Urge students to be supportive of more community-wide efforts to make the world more beautiful. Get permission from the local parks and recreation office to host a cleanup day in the spring. Try to arrange a field trip to a park in need of help. After collecting trash and raking leaves, paint a welcome banner to display and, of course, plant some wildflower or lupine seeds. After a lunch break, relax with a rereading of *Miss Rumphius.* Like little Alice and Miss Rumphius, your students will be planting more than flower seeds, they'll be planting the seed of community service.

> ## Rich Vocabulary
>
> **wandered** *v.*
> walked around slowly

Name _____ Date _____

Mice Math

Directions: Color and cut out the Seven Blind Mice. Glue yarn for their tails. Use the mice to help you solve number sentences on the Strange Something Story Mat.

Use with *Seven Blind Mice* by Ed Young.

Teaching With Favorite Read-Alouds in First Grade

The Strange Something Story Mat

Directions: Create number stories for the Seven Blind Mice.

Place mice on the story mat to show your stories.

Use with *Seven Blind Mice* by Ed Young.

Chapter 5:
Purple Coats, Purple Purses, Typing Cows, and Talking Dogs

10 Must-Have Books for Teaching Reading and Writing

Chapter Objectives:

* ✳ practicing speaking and listening skills
* ✳ editing written work for punctuation and descriptive language
* ✳ using conventions of spelling in written compositions
* ✳ using phonemic spelling to convey basic ideas
* ✳ using descriptive language to convey basic ideas
* ✳ exploring the writing process
* ✳ relating stories to personal experience
* ✳ using structural analysis to identify words with −ed and −ing endings
* ✳ increasing vocabulary awareness
* ✳ sharing great books to inspire student writing

A book-based classroom puts literature at center stage. For first graders at the height of reading readiness, being surrounded by printed material is critical in taking the first steps into the world of reading. A great book is evidence to children that words have meaning, that reading is an important skill to learn, and that writing well is a task worth doing.

To make writing more detailed, teach the add-a-word trick after reading *The Relatives Came*. Study plural endings with *Frederick*. Explore synonyms with *Dr. DeSoto* and quotation marks with *Martha Speaks*. Edit stories with *Author: A True Story*. Let the wordless *Frog, Where Are You?* emphasize the importance of the sequence of events in a story. Use *Click Clack Moo* to introduce a spelling center. *The Purple Coat* provides a great example of writing style. Study words ending in −ed with *When I Was Young in the Mountains*. *Lilly's Purple Plastic Purse* is filled with reading and writing tricks of the trade.

---

10 Must-Have Books for Teaching Reading and Writing

The Relatives Came by Cynthia Rylant

Frederick by Leo Lionni

Dr. DeSoto by William Steig

Martha Speaks by Susan Meddaugh

Author: A True Story by Helen Lester

Frog, Where Are You? by Mercer Mayer

Click Clack Moo by Doreen Cronin

The Purple Coat by Amy Hest

When I Was Young in the Mountains by Cynthia Rylant

Lilly's Purple Plastic Purse by Kevin Henkes

The Relatives Came
by Cynthia Rylant

LEARNING ABOUT Using Descriptive Language

It was difficult going to sleep with all that new breathing in the house.
— From *The Relatives Came*, page 19

Thus begins the description of the first night when the relatives came—and then went to bed. This sentence allows readers to hear the new breathing that makes sleeping troublesome and to feel the excitement of visitors in the house. Similarly, being hugged against "wrinkled Virginia clothes" adds a sense of touch to the story, while the phrase "almost purple grapes" paints a picture with words.

Adding one descriptive word is an effective technique for making stories sound more like real authors' stories, and it's not intimidating to students. This add-a-word trick makes writing with descriptive language appealing to young writers. In the mini-lesson that follows, we highlight the extra words used by Cynthia Rylant in *The Relatives Came* to prove how powerful this extra effort can be. Which paints a better picture—sandwiches or bologna sandwiches? grapes or almost purple grapes? clothes or wrinkled Virginia clothes?

Before beginning the read-aloud and mini-lesson, make copies

Rich Vocabulary

reunion *n.* a get-together after being apart for a while

of the reproducible on page 93 so students can record the add-a-word tricks used in the book. Here's how the lesson unfolds in my classroom.

Mrs. L.:	Close your eyes. I'm going to say a word, and I want you to picture what I say. Ready? *Grapes.* Tell me what you imagine. What do the grapes look like?
Josh:	Yellow.
Madeline:	I pictured purple ones.
William:	I saw blackish-purple ones.
Emily:	Mine were seedless.
Mrs. L.:	I guess I should have been more specific in my description. Close your eyes again. This time I'll add a word or two: *reddish-purple grapes.* Now what do you see?
Class:	Reddish-purple grapes.
Mrs. L.:	Exactly! That one word certainly made a difference in what you imagined, didn't it? I call this the add-a-word trick. It's a trick writers use for painting pictures with words. Cynthia Rylant is an expert at the add-a-word trick. She used it eleven times in telling the story of *The Relatives Came.* Adding just one word or two gives greater description and detail to a story. For me, these few extra words often make the difference between what is a favorite and a not-so favorite book.
Joey:	It means she had to write more words.
Mrs. L.:	You're right, and I think it was worth it. I'll reread the story while you focus on finding the added words Cynthia Rylant used to describe certain things in the story. I've listed the main words on this recording sheet. Your job is to find the extra words she added and write them on the blanks.
Casey:	Can we use sound-spelling?
Mrs. L.:	Absolutely. The first added word you'll be looking for is used to describe the word *car.*
Travis:	I can see from the book cover that it's a colorful car.
Jacob:	It's a speeding car.
Grace:	And a packed-full car.
Mrs. L.:	These are all excellent words to describe the relatives' car. All your ideas add details to the story. Let's read to see which word Cynthia Rylant used to describe the car: "It was in the summer of the year when the relatives came. They came up from Virginia. They left when their grapes were nearly purple enough to pick, but not quite. They had an old station wagon that smelled like a real car, and in it—"
Madeline:	*Real!* It was a real car! It smelled like a real car.
Mrs. L.:	What an interesting description of the car.
Daniel:	What does a real car smell like?
Greg:	Probably like a new car. Or it smelled like gasoline or something like that.
Billy:	I think real means it was used a lot, and it smelled like food. Didn't they have sandwiches in the car? That's our next word.
Mrs. L.:	I'll keep reading: ". . . and in it they put an ice chest full of soda pop and some boxes of crackers and some bologna sandwiches, and up they came"—

Makenzie:	*Bologna* is the added word. They weren't peanut butter and jelly sandwiches, they were bologna.
Christy:	I can spell that—*b-a-l-o-n-e-e.*
Mrs. L.:	Good sound-spelling. It's spelled *b-o-l-o-g-n-a* in the book. You can use sound-spelling if you like. When I spell *bologna*, I say "ba-log-na" to myself so I spell it correctly.
Vince:	It looks like *ba-log-na.*
Brooke:	I'm glad Cynthia Rylant added *bologna* to *sandwiches.* It paints a better picture.
Mrs. L.:	I agree. The next word you're looking for is—
Class:	*Houses.*
Bobby:	Then *mountains.*
Mrs. L.:	Keep listening: "They left at four in the morning when it was still dark, before even the birds were awake. They drove all day long and into the night, and while they traveled along they looked at the strange houses and different mountains"—
Katie:	Strange houses—
Sara:	And different mountains!
Daniel:	I don't think it means weird houses for *strange*, it's just ones they've never seen before. This must be their first trip to their relatives' house.
William:	Or maybe they go a lot, but they aren't the kind of houses and mountains they see in Virginia, so they look strange and different when they pass them.
Mrs. L.:	Good thinking! These words, *strange* and *different*, let you imagine what it must be like for the relatives driving along. Everything looks new so they're taking it all in as they ride along.
Madeline:	I think the grapes part is coming up next. There are two added words for grapes. I remember them.
Mrs. L.:	I'll read on: "and they thought about their almost purple grapes back home"—
Madeline:	Almost purple! That's my favorite added word.
Brooke:	It's two words. I can really picture that.
Mrs. L.:	Go ahead and write *almost purple* next to *grapes.* The next few lines are my favorites. *(We continue reading and then students add the words* wrinkled Virginia *to* clothes.*)*
Jeannie:	I can imagine what being hugged against wrinkled Virginia clothes must be like.
Casey:	They would be really wrinkled since they drove all those miles in the car.
Mrs. L.:	What kind of faces do you think we'll read about next?
Jacob:	Smiling faces.
Makenzie:	Friendly faces.
Peter:	Happy-teared faces.
Mrs. L.:	Great ideas. Let's see what Cynthia Rylant added for detail. *(We continue to read.)*
Katie:	Shining faces! She wrote *shining.*
Jacob:	That means "smiling."
Makenzie:	And friendly.
Katie:	I like *shining*. It lets you know they're really happy.

Teaching With Favorite Read-Alouds in First Grade

Mrs. L.:	It's a different word from what you'd expect and that makes it special, too. What kind of talk do you think we'll discover when we continue reading?
Emily:	Catching-up talk. Because they haven't had a chance to talk to each other in a long time.
Mrs. L.:	I like that idea.
Josh:	What about happy talk? They might be talking about how much they've grown—my aunt always does that.
Daniel:	I bet it's loud. There are a lot of relatives talking.
Mrs. L.:	Let's see. *(I continue to read.)*
Joey:	Quiet talk! Even though there were a lot of relatives talking, they were quiet. Maybe they were too full from all that food to talk too loudly.
Mrs. L.:	Maybe. The idea of quiet talk gives a relaxing mood to the story. Like you said, Joey, they're filled with supper, they're catching up on what's happening, they're happy, and everyone is involved in quiet conversations all around the house.
Sara:	It's also been a long trip so the relatives are probably a little tired.
Mrs. L.:	I think so, too. The next word used to describe breathing is one of my favorites. When I read this book the first time, I knew it was going to be a favorite when I read this line.
Makenzie:	New breathing! I remember it from the first time you read it to us.
Greg:	I do, too. She's right. It is new breathing. They aren't sure how they're ever going to go to sleep because of all the snoring.
Emily:	Not snoring, just different people breathing differently.
Grace:	And there's extra excitement because of all the relatives sharing the house with them. I bet that little girl is never going to fall asleep!
Mrs. L.:	My daughter, Maddie, would be like that. She's always too excited to sleep when her cousin, Sarah, comes to visit. Let's keep reading. It's almost time for the relatives to go back to Virginia. We're looking for a word to describe grapes again.
Vince:	We already wrote *almost purple*.
Madeline:	This time it's not going to be almost purple. *(I continue to read.)*
Grace:	It's dark purple! Now the

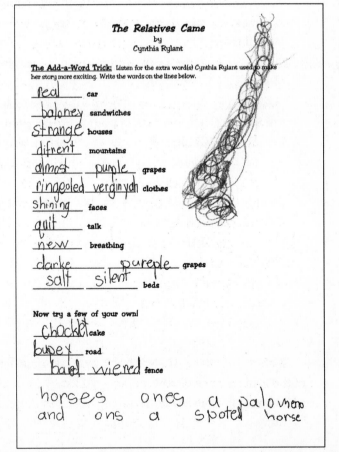

grapes are more than just plain purple, they are dark purple.

Mrs. L.: I like that. It shows how time has passed.

Madeline: The relatives are almost home again. Here's the last page: "And when they were finally home in Virginia, they crawled into their silent, soft beds and dreamed about next summer."

Sara: "Silent, soft beds." They don't have any "new breathing" anymore. It's all the same old breathing.

Mrs. L.: I want to give you a chance to try out the add-a-word trick for yourselves. I think we would all agree that "wrinkled Virginia clothes" sounds more exciting than just plain clothes, and "shining faces" is more detailed than just plain faces. "Silent, soft beds" gives us a different feeling than plain beds. Let's give the add-a-word trick a try for the words *cake* and *day*.

My class came up with the following phrases:

CAKE	DAY
thunder cake	jacket day
chocolate cake	hot summer vacation day
lemon cake	sticky summery day
banana cake	white snowy day
polka-dot cake	blow-your-hat-off day
crumbling cake	Popsicle day
melt-in-your mouth cake	dark stormy day

Next, I let students work with partners to brainstorm added words for *chair, walk,* or *road.*

CHAIR	WALK	ROAD
soft comfy chair	listening walk	bumpy road
overstuffed chair	talking walk	smooth road
well-loved chair	thinking walk	rocky road
green striped chair	dog walk	Dark Horse Road
book reading chair	fall day walk	popcorn road
snuggling chair	I'm late walk	dusty road
rocking chair	looking walk	potholed road
Dad's chair	happy walk	yellow brick road
cat's chair	drag your feet walk	
sick day chair		
Gee Gee's chair		

With the books we share in the future, we discuss other examples of this technique. The results of this activity arm the students with a strategy for enriching details in the stories they write by adding one or more words. By doing this, even beginning writers can write like the experts.

More Must-Have Books for Teaching Reading and Writing

Frederick
by Leo Lionni

Identifying Words with Plural Endings

While the other mice work day and night gathering nuts and corn and wheat and straw, Frederick is busy collecting his own supplies: sun rays for the cold dark winter days, colors for gray winter days, and words for long winter days when the mice run out of things to say. Although the mice are doubtful, when the nuts and corn and straw and wheat are but a memory, Frederick's voice works magic to warm them and brighten their days as he entertains them with poetry.

This classic story entertains first graders, too, who, like the four field mice, applaud Frederick's efforts at the end of the story. For an interactive listening center based on this entertaining book, make an audio recording of *Frederick* during your read-aloud. As students listen to the story at the center during independent work time, they can record the 25+ words with plural endings in the text. (Provide an answer key so students can check their work.)

During a group gathering time, discuss how words like *cows* and *potatoes* have –s and -es endings to show that they're plural. Explain that some words, however, change in different ways to show more than one: *mouse* becomes *mice*, not *mouses*; *foot* becomes *feet*, not *foots*.

Rich Vocabulary

applauded *v.*
clapped

MORE FUN WITH THE BOOK

For illustrating fun, let students give Leo Lionni's torn-paper collage technique a try. Hand out construction paper and glue sticks for students to make a torn-paper field mouse to decorate their recording pages. After students tear the body shape, they cut out ears, eyes, arms, legs, and a tail and attach them with glue.

TEACHING TIP

You may also need to talk about verbs with –s endings, for instance, *scatters, spoils, dims,* and *comes.* Remind students that plural –s and –es endings make a word mean "more than one." Although these words clearly end in –s, this added letter does not mean more than one.

Dr. DeSoto
by William Steig

Recognizing Synonyms

Rich Vocabulary

whimper *v.* to cry out, perhaps in pain

remarkable *adj.* very special, worth noticing

In this Newberry Honor Book, we meet the clever Dr. DeSoto and his dental assistant, who also happens to be his wife. The DeSotos devise a plan to outfox the fox who has plans to eat them when his dental work is complete. "Raw with salt, indeed," mutters Doctor DeSoto. "How foolish to trust a fox!" First graders hang on to every word and giggle with delight at the ending sentence where the DeSotos "kissed each other and took the rest of the day off."

Since William Steig is a wordsmith worthy of replicating, revisit *Dr. DeSoto* for a word study lesson on synonyms for *said*. Duplicate the reproducible on page 94. As you reread the story, have students record the 16 words William Steig uses in place of *said*, and make a tally mark to show the limited number of times that word is used as well. Discuss how the variety of words gives greater detail to the story as *gasped, announced, wailed,* and *shouted,* for example, have distinctly different meanings than simply saying something.

Synonyms for *said* in Dr. De Soto include *shouted, wailed, whispered, cried, gasped, announced, whimpered, yelled, mumbled, yelped, muttered, wondered, chortled, exclaimed, thought, declared.*

ON ANOTHER DAY
After reading all the ways Dr. DeSoto said things, have your students revisit a piece of their own writing and edit synonyms for *said*.

Martha Speaks
by Susan Meddaugh

Using Quotation Marks

The day Helen gave Martha dog her alphabet soup, something unusual happened. The letters in the soup went up to Martha's brain instead of down to her stomach. That evening, Martha spoke.
— From *Martha Speaks,* pages 3–5

If I knew my dogs would talk after eating alphabet soup, I'd have to think twice about giving it to them—especially after reading what Martha has to say. I know my dog, Jordan, would have a lot to tell us about his puppy days at a Penn State fraternity house prior to his running away and eventually being adopted by us: "I had pizza every night at the frat house. And the boys didn't make a big deal if I mistook the dining room table leg for a tree. Ever since I moved in with you, it's nothing but rules, rules, rules. No eating frozen steaks off the counter, no shredding pillows, no chewing on the furniture or those giant dog toys you call kids' toys, no eating the cat—where is that fat furball anyway? Rules, rules, rules."

Take advantage of Martha's talkative nature with a lesson on quotation marks. A talking dog certainly makes for an appealing lesson. To help students practice using quotation marks, write the words that Susan Meddaugh has Martha say in the speech balloons. Encourage students to use the synonyms for *said* from the Dr. DeSoto lesson to help finish Martha's sentences, and to add quotation marks and change the ending punctuation when necessary. Practice a sentence or two like the following with your class:

Hello. Acme Meat Company? I'd like to make an order.

"Hello. Acme Meat Company? I'd like to make an order," Martha whispered into the phone.

Wanna go for a walk, Granny?

"Wanna go for a walk, Granny?" Martha asked after dinner.

Let students choose a few sentences from the following list to try on their own:

- *How's the flea problem?*
- *Please pass the carcass.*
- *How much do I owe you?*
- *WOOF! Just kidding.*
- *Mom said that fruitcake you sent wasn't fit for a dog. But I thought it was delicious.*
- *Helen did it.*

ON ANOTHER DAY

During writers' workshop, have Martha host a mini-lesson on other clever words that might come out of dogs' mouths. Reinforce quotation mark usage, careful sound-spelling, and creative writing as Martha motivates your first graders to write a story from a dog's—or cat's or bird's or hamster's—perspective. To get writing started, copy the beginning sentence from *Martha Speaks* followed by the ideas you generated together. Some examples are shown below.

The day Helen gave Martha dog her alphabet soup, something unusual happened.

Words From the Mouths of Dogs
- *"Where have you been all day? I missed you soooooo much," Sydney yelped as her tail thumped against the closed front door.*
- *"Get away from my kids." Tucker barked a warning as a stranger approached.*
- *"Have you been around another dog?" Abby sniffed anxiously.*

- *"I wanna go to the park. I wanna go to the park," Omar whined.*
- *"I don't want to go to the vet!" Casey cried as she ran under the couch.*
- *"Daddy's home!" Keri exclaimed as she jumped off the ground with excitement.*
- *"Could I have steak tonight?" Max begged. "This dog food is getting a little stale."*
- *"Just give me one little tiny bite of pizza, pleeeeease!" Jordan whimpered.*

Author: A True Story
by Helen Lester

 **LEARNING ABOUT** **Introducing the Writing Process**

Usually when I first think a book is finished, it really isn't. I keep going over the story again and again, looking for ways to make it better with little changes here and there. I do this until the book has to be printed. Then it's too late to do anything more!
— From *Author: A True Story*, page 26

This book is a must-have for every primary writers' workshop. Share this true account of one author's growth from the best three-year-old grocery list writer in the world to a real, better-than-a-dream-come-true author. Discuss the author's disappointments and triumphs, and watch as your young writers relax. Helen Lester comforts young writers (and older ones) as she laughs at her own writing struggles in this guide for young readers and writers. Keep this book handy for it will be used again and again as your young writers encounter problems in their own writing.

To introduce the writing process to my young writers, I begin by rereading the above quote. Then I share the beginning of a story of my own, and together, the students and I edit it in a similar fashion to the Lester's process shown on page 27 of her book. Then students tackle stories of their own.

> **Rich Vocabulary**
>
> **persist** *v.* to keep trying

~~The Hungry Yellow Lab~~
Dinner Time for Buddy
by Mrs. L.
~~The yellow Lab was hungry.~~ *Nope.*
~~The yellow Lab barked three barks as if to say I am hungry.~~ *Nope.*
The yellow Lab dragged his bowl across the room to me and barked three barks.
"Are you hungry, Buddy?" I asked.
He wagged his tail and nudged the bowl closer to me.

The Kite That Got Away
by Christy
~~*I lik to fli kites.*~~
It was a prfct day to fling my new orang kite. The wind was ~~*prfct jently*~~ *bloing strong enuf for my kite to* ~~*go*~~ *lift into the air.*

During writers' workshop, I look for editing examples from the students' writing and ask them to share their changes during story sharing time.

More Book-Based Mini-Lesson Ideas

1. Illustrate the publishing process as shown below (adapted from *Literature Based Mini-Lessons to Teach Writing* by Susan Lunsford, Scholastic Professional Books, 1998, page 115). (Also see the book for more book-based lessons for *Author: A True Story*.)
2. Write grocery lists to practice sound-spelling.
3. Make a class Fizzle Box.
4. Draw a diagram showing the writing process for a "perfect book." (Refer to pages 22–23 of *Author: A True Story*.)
5. Create a list of story starters to hang in the writing center for students to use when "writing is hard."
6. Talk about what to do if . . .
   - you're stuck (Ask a friend to listen to the story and offer suggestions or peruse a favorite book.)
   - you can't think of a title (Ask fellow writers for suggestions or look through the classroom library.)
   - you have trouble making editorial changes (See the editor.)
   - you lose your pencils (Get another one from the writing center.)
   - you get frustrated and feel like giving up on a story (Talk it over with fellow writers; read a favorite book and be glad that that author didn't give up.)

THE WRITING PROCESS

1. Think of a great idea.
2. Use this idea to write a really great story. Make sure the story has the following:
   - a great beginning
   - a strong middle
   - an ending with a last sentence that brings the story together
   - words that paint pictures
3. Read the story with a friend.
4. Make changes.
5. Share the story with the editor (teacher).
6. Make more changes.
7. Add the following finishing touches:
   - a fancy cover
   - a dedication page
   - an About the Author page
8. Share your edited story with an audience.

Teaching With Favorite Read-Alouds in First Grade

Frog, Where Are You?

by Mercer Mayer

LEARNING ABOUT Sequencing Events

In this sequel to *A Boy, a Dog and a Frog,* a boy and a dog go looking for a frog—unfortunately, they're looking in all the wrong places. He's not in the hole in the ground, but the groundhog is. He's not in the beehive, but the bees are. He's not in the hole in the tree, but the owl is. Maybe if the boy stands on a tree branch—wait, that's not a tree branch, it's a buck and he's carrying the boy away!

First graders (and their teachers) begin turning the pages of this irresistible book and "forget that it's wordless," as Jeannie remarked in class one day. Master author and illustrator Mercer Mayer needs no words to tell this story. It's easy reading for young children of all ages and abilities, delightful for the most advanced readers in the class, and a confidence builder for the less capable ones.

Wordless books are must-haves for first-grade classrooms, and this one should be at the top of the list. They give all beginning readers a break from trying to crack the reading code while reinforcing prereading and oral language skills. By using picture clues, figuring out what makes sense, and looking for details, *Frog, Where Are You?* is perfect for first-grade classroom libraries. The comically illustrated pictures will inspire many rereadings as the action-filled pictures seem to move from page to page.

After rereading this book, write a class story based on the main events. Make a list of questions the boy might ask his dog as they search for their favorite friend, Frog. Have students practice using capital letters and question marks at the end of each sentence. The list of questions my students and I generated looked something like this:

Where did Frog go?
How did he get out of the jar?
Frog, where are you?
Are you in that hole in the ground?
Are you in that hole in the tree?
Frog, where are you?
Are you in the pond?
Are you behind the log?
Do you mind if we take care of one of your babies, Frog?

Encourage various retellings of the story by pairs of students. Have one partner take the part of the boy and the other partner respond as the dog. An oral story may begin something like this:

Rich Vocabulary

determined *adj.*
make up one's mind to do something

Boy:	Goodnight, Frog. Come on, Dog, time for bed.
Dog:	Goodnight, little frog.
Boy and Dog:	ZZZZzzzzzz.
Dog:	Wake up, Boy! Frog is gone!
Boy:	What? How did he get out of the jar? Quick! He can't be far. I'll check inside my boot.
Dog:	I'll check the jar again.
Boy:	FROG, WHERE ARE YOU?
Dog:	Uh-oh! HELP! (crash) Lick. Lick. Lick.
Boy:	You silly Dog!

Pairs of students will enjoy performing their versions of *Frog, Where Are You?* for classmates.

....

Click Clack Moo
by Doreen Cronin

**"Cows that type. Hens on strike! Whoever heard of such a thing?
How can I run a farm with no milk and no eggs!" Farmer Brown was furious.**
— From *Click, Clack, Moo: Cows That Type*, page 19

Like Farmer Brown, I am shocked that his cows can type. But as a teacher, I am quite impressed with their spelling ability! What excellent book-spelling these cows use. As I made this comment to my class, one student noticed the cows even spelled *electric* and *sincerely* correctly. And, I add, they use proper punctuation, too. Don't forget their vocabulary. *Exchange* and *boring* are pretty big words for cows and ducks to use.

Children love this comically written book that depicts the animals' strike against chilly working conditions at Farmer Brown's farm. With every click clack moo, click clack moo, clickety clack moo, the animals grow more determined, and students' smiles get wider.

Give them a chance to click clack, type and be "Kids That Spell." After reading this book, set up a typing center where children can sharpen their spelling skills.

Reread a few of the simple notes from the cows and ducks to Farmer Brown, and then write a letter of reply together. Display the charted responses near a typewriter or a computer keyboard for everyone to see. Here is one of our responses.

Rich Vocabulary

exchange *v.* to trade

Teaching With Favorite Read-Alouds in First Grade

Dear Cows and Hens:
There will be no electric blankets. You are cows and hens.
I demand milk and eggs.
Sincerely,
Farmer Brown

Students will be happily clicking and clacking—perhaps letter by letter—and getting some spelling reinforcement, letter recognition, and letter-writing and keyboard practice. When introducing the typing center, be sure to explain to students how to use the space bar between words. If you're using typewriters, show how to touch the return key at the end of lines.

ON ANOTHER DAY

Students may wish to write letters from other farm friends who make demands of Farmer Brown or congratulation notes to the cows, hens, and ducks. Or how about thank-you notes to Farmer Brown from his well-spelled barnyard crew?

Dear Farmer Brown,
Thank you for the warm and cozy electric blankets. We use them every night.
Sincerely,
The Cows and Ducks
P.S. You might be hearing from the pigs soon. They asked to borrow the typewriter.

The Purple Coat
by Amy Hest

 **Using Descriptive Language**

"Now business." Grampa brushes crumbs off the knees of his pants and points to a half dozen bolts of dark fabric. "I've pulled all the navy blues. Dark and lighter, nearly sapphire, smoky navy, hazy navy—"
"I want purple." Gabby interrupts.
"Purple? But you always get a navy coat!"
"This time I want purple."
— From *The Purple Coat*, pages 18

The Purple Coat is a book that gets a lot of mileage in my classroom—from math, word study, conflict resolution, and social studies connections to writers' workshop mini-lessons. Every page is filled with descriptive language, the characters show rather than tell their feelings, and the story

> **Rich Vocabulary**
>
> **compromise** *n.*
> working together
> to solve a problem
> so that everyone
> is happy

problem and ending resolution are perfect for every child who, like Gabby, ever felt that "once in a while, it's good to try something new."

After reading and discussing the story, both text and illustrations, I bring the book to many writers' workshop mini-lessons. There is an endless list of skills and techniques for young writers to gain from *The Purple Coat*. When I notice a few of my students trying to emulate Amy Hest's writing style, I reread the story, pausing to discuss the extra tweaks and little touches she adds that make her style so unique. We attempt to get at the heart of what makes her writing style so impressive. What prompts us to want to read this story over and over, each time finding new favorite sentences?

Then we meet on the carpet for a lesson on character observation. I begin by asking the class to look at the illustrations in the book as they retell the story of *The Purple Coat* in their minds. As they do, I jot down small observations of my young characters as they silently revisit the story:

Josh: adjusts his glasses
Emily: scratches her arm
William: reties his shoe
Madeline: smoothes her skirt
Casey: smiles as she remembers
Travis: eyebrows jut up in surprise
Grace: bites her lip to hold back words
Billy: wrinkles up his nose
Makenzie: twirls her hair around a finger

After I share these observations, we talk about how writers must always be looking and thinking of little details to make stories more enjoyable. We reread a few selected pages of *The Purple Coat* and pause to list the little touches that Amy Hest has included in this great book.
- "nose pressed to the smudge-glass" (page 6)
- "pulls her gray rag socks just past her knees" (page 11)
- "puffing out her lower lip" (page 11)
- "slips her left foot into and out of the fringed moccasin" (page 12)
- "drags red-painted fingertips, slowly" (page 14)
- "rubs a fist across the pointy part of his chin" (page 21)
- "clicks two fingers in the air" (page 22)
- "Grampa stands a little taller" (page 22)
- "Gabby jumps high in the air" (page 22)
- "When she lands, her socks are scrunched around her ankles." (page 22)
- "Gabby twirls in front of the dusty mirror." (page 26)
- "Grampa clears his throat." (page 26)

Next, we take a few minutes to look at and think about our surroundings from a writer's perspective. Armed with pencils, paper, listening ears, and writers' eyes, I invite my young writers to jot down observations of classmates. Encouraged by Amy Hest's little touches of detail, still fresh in their minds, the students are eager to share their discoveries.

Daniel: She dropped her pencil, eraser-end down.
Christy: Jacob looked like he was going to sneeze.
Vince: Billy's pencil erased loudly.
Joey: She tapped her pencil on the desk about 100 times.
Casey: Brooke raised her eyebrows when she got an idea.
Emily: Katie's mouth moved but no words came out.

During writers' workshop sharing time, the students read their own sentences with little touches of detail that *show* rather than *tell* the audience what a character is feeling.

Sparky paced back and forth sixteen times.
Gabby put the sandwich back on the plate. She just couldn't eat it.
The team walked slowly off the field.
She wagged her tail till it almost fell off.
Gramma patted Dora's head and smiled.

(For more lessons based on *The Purple Coat* by Amy Hest, see *100 Skill-Building Lessons Using 10 Favorite Books* by Susan Lunsford, Scholastic Professional Books, 2001.)

··

When I Was Young in the Mountains
by Cynthia Rylant

 **LEARNING ABOUT** **Words Ending In -*ed* and -*ing***

When I was young in the mountains,
Grandfather came home in the evening
covered with the black dust of a coal mine.
Only his lips were clean, and he used them
to kiss the top of my head.

— From *When I Was Young in the Mountains,* page 4

Rich Vocabulary

draped *v.* wrapped around

threaten *v.* to warn

This Caldecott Honor book is a beautifully written and illustrated account of growing up simply with a johnny-house, okra for dinner, a dark and muddy swimming hole, and tin tubs filled with water pumped from a well for baths.

Revisit this book, and let Cynthia Rylant's words help with a lesson on -*ed* and -*ing* endings. As the author writes about the past, she uses many words with -*ed* endings to tell about the things the family did in the story. She also uses some words that end in -*ing* to tell what characters were doing when they were young in the mountains. Have students listen to the story and write down all the words they hear that end in -*ed* and -*ing*. Encourage good sound-spelling!

Lilly's Purple Plastic Purse

by Kevin Henkes

LEARNING ABOUT   Relating Stories to Personal Experiences

Working at the Lightbulb Lab

*Whenever the students had free time, they were permitted to go to the
Lightbulb Lab in the back of the classroom.
They expressed their ideas creatively through drawing and writing.
Lilly went often.
She had a lot of ideas . . .*

— From *Lilly's Purple Plastic Purse*, page 9

First graders, like Lilly, have lots of ideas and need
suggestions for using free time wisely. After reading and
discussing *Lilly's Purple Plastic Purse* for a read-aloud, set up a
Lightbulb Lab for your students where
"great ideas are born." Fill a purse (purple
and plastic, if possible) with index cards of
activities based on this great book. When
students have free time, they can choose
an activity card from the purse and work
on a project to "wow" their teacher, as
Lilly "wows" Mr. Slinger. Here are a few
creative ways for your students to express
their ideas.

Lilly wants to be a teacher
when she grows up.

Write a story about what
you want to be when you
grow up.

Mr. Slinger and the students
were making a list of words
that rhyme with <u>mice</u>.

Make a list of rhyming
words of your own.

If you had a purple plastic
purse or book bag, what
would you put inside it?

Draw a picture. Label it.

Kevin Henkes drew a picture
to show Lilly furious at Mr.
Slinger.

Draw a picture of yourself
feeling furious. Write about
what made you feel this way.

Lilly drew a picture of Mr.
Slinger and wrote a story
about him, too.

Write a story and a picture
about your teacher.

The Add-a-Word Trick

Directions: Cynthia Rylant uses extra words to make *The Relatives Came* more exciting. Listen for these extra words. Write them on the lines below.

_____ car

_____ sandwiches

_____ houses

_____ mountains

_____ _____ grapes

_____ _____ clothes

_____ faces

_____ talk

_____ breathing

_____ _____ grapes

_____ _____ beds

Now try a few of your own.

_____ chair

_____ walk

_____ _____ road

Use with *The Relatives Came* by Cynthia Rylant.

A synonym is a word that means the same or almost the same as another word.

Dr. DeSoto's Synonyms

Directions: Author William Steig is an expert on words that mean the same as *said*. Listen to *Dr. DeSoto*. Then write down all the synonyms for *said* that you hear. Write a tally mark each time the author uses *said*.

1. _____   9. _____

2. _____   10. _____

3. _____   11. _____

4. _____   12. _____

5. _____   13. _____

6. _____   14. _____

7. _____   15. _____

8. _____   16. _____

said: _____

Use with *Dr. DeSoto* by William Steig.

Teaching With Favorite Read-Alouds in First Grade

50 Must-Have Books for First Grade

Ackerman, Karen. *Song and Dance Man.* New York: Alfred A. Knopf, 1988.

Brown, Marc. *Arthur's Birthday.* Boston: Little, Brown and Company, 1989.

——. *Arthur's Teacher Trouble.* Boston: Little, Brown and Company, 1986.

Bunting, Eve. *Night Tree.* New York: Harcourt Brace & Company, 1991.

Cannon, Janell. *Stellaluna.* New York: Harcourt Brace, 1993.

Carle, Eric. *The Grouchy Ladybug.* New York: HarperCollins Publishers, 1977.

Cazet, Denys. *Never Spit on Your Shoes.* New York: Orchard Books, 1990.

Cooney, Barbara. *Miss Rumphius.* New York: Viking Penguin, 1982.

Cronin, Doreen. *Click Clack Moo.* New York: Simon & Schuster Books for Young Readers, 2000.

dePaola, Tomie. *The Art Lesson.* New York: G.P. Putnam's Sons, 1989.

Ehlert, Lois. *Feathers for Lunch.* New York: Harcourt Brace & Company, 1990.

Finchler, Judy. *Miss Malarkey Doesn't Live in Room 10.* New York: Walker Publishing Company, 1995.

Henkes, Kevin. *Chrysanthemum.* New York: Greenwillow Books, 1991.

——. *Lilly's Purple Plastic Purse.* New York: William Morrow & Company, 1996.

——. *A Weekend with Wendell.* New York: Greenwillow Books, 1986.

Hest, Amy. *The Purple Coat.* New York: Macmillan Publishing Company, 1992.

Hopkins, Lee Bennett. *Good Books, Good Times.* New York: HarperCollins Juvenile Books, 2000.

Kellogg, Steven. *Best Friends.* New York: Dial Books for Young Readers, 1986.

Kirk, David. *Miss Spider's Tea Party.* New York: Scholastic, 1994.

Kraus, Robert. *Leo the Late Bloomer.* New York: Windmill Books, 1971.

Lester, Helen. *Author: A True Story.* Boston: Houghton Mifflin Company, 1997.

Lewis, J. Patrick. *A Hippopotamusn't.* New York: Dial Books for Young Readers, 1990.

Lionni, Leo. *Frederick.* New York: Alfred A. Knopf, 1967.

Lobel, Arnold. *Frog and Toad Are Friends.* New York: Harper & Row, 1970.

Mahy, Margaret. *17 Kings and 42 Elephants.* New York: Dial Books for Young Readers, 1972.

Martin, Bill, Jr. and Archambault, John. *Knots on a Counting Rope.* New York: Henry Holt and Company, 1987.

Mayer, Mercer. *Frog, Where Are You?* New York: Dial Books for Young Readers, 1969.

Meddaugh, Susan. *Martha Speaks.* Boston: Houghton Mifflin Company, 1992.

Moss, Lloyd. *Zin! Zin! Zin! A Violin.* New York: Simon & Schuster, 1995.

Noble, Trinka Hakes. *Jimmy's Boa and the Big Splash Birthday Bash.* New York: Dial Books for Young Readers, 1989.

Polacco, P. *Thank You, Mr. Falker.* New York: Philomel Books, 1998.

——. *Thunder Cake.* New York: The Putnam & Grosset Group, 1990.

Prelutsky, Jack. *Something BIG Has Been Here.* New York: Greenwillow Books, 1990.

Rylant, Cynthia. *The Bookshop Dog.* New York: The Blue Sky Press, 1996.

——. *The Relatives Came.* New York: Simon & Schuster Children's Publishing, 1985.

——. *When I Was Young in the Mountains.* New York: E.P. Dutton, 1982.

Schwartz, David, M. *How Much Is a Million?* New York: Lothrop, Lee & Shepard Books, 1985.

Shannon, David. *David Goes to School.* New York: Scholastic, 1999.

Silverstein, Shel. *Where the Sidewalk Ends.* New York: HarperCollins Publishers, 1974.

Steig, William. *Dr. DeSoto.* New York: Farrar, Straus and Giroux, 1982.

Stevens, Janet. *Tops and Bottoms.* New York: Harcourt Brace & Company, 1995.

Taback, Simms. *There Was An Old Lady Who Swallowed a Fly.* New York: Viking, 1997.

Van Allsburg, Chris. *The Polar Express.* Boston: Houghton Mifflin Company, 1985.

Viorst, Judith. *Alexander and the Terrible, Horrible, No Good, Very Bad Day.* New York: Atheneum Books for Young Readers, 1972.

Wells, Rosemary. *Emily's First 100 Days of School.* New York: Hyperion Books for Children, 2000.

——. *Noisy Nora.* New York: Dial Books for Young Readers, 1997.

——. *Yoko.* New York: Hyperion Books for Children, 1998.

Williams, Vera. *A Chair for My Mother.* New York: Greenwillow Press, 1982.

Yolen, Jane. *Owl Moon.* New York: The Putnam Publishing Group, 1987.

Young, Ed. *Seven Blind Mice.* New York: Philomel Books, 1992.

Grade 1 Learning Skills

Reading with fluency and expression
Miss Spider's Tea Party, pp. 51–52
The Polar Express, p. 36

Reading strategies
Making inferences:
A Weekend with Wendell, p. 29
Sequence:
Frog, Where Are You?, pp. 87–88
There Was an Old Lady Who Swallowed a Fly, pp. 56–57

Relating stories and poems to personal experience
Alexander and the Terrible, Horrible, No Good, Very Bad Day, pp. 34–35
Good Books, Good Times, pp. 55–56
Lilly's Purple Plastic Purse, p. 92
Thank You, Mr. Falker, pp. 21–22
Classroom rules:
David Goes to School, p. 19
Setting goals:
Leo the Late Bloomer, pp. 18–19

Writing in a variety of genres
Invitations:
Jimmy's Boa and the Big Splash Birthday Bash, p. 28
Letters:
Arthur's Birthday, p. 30
Click Clack Moo, pp. 88–89
Lists:
Song and Dance Man, p. 37
Preparing work for display:
The Art Lesson, pp. 31–32
Writing about a favorite poem:
A Hippopotamusn't, p. 52

Writing process
Author: A True Story, pp. 85–86

Spelling conventions
17 Kings and 42 Elephants, pp. 44–47
Arthur's Teacher Trouble, pp. 16–17
Never Spit on Your Shoes, p. 20
Something BIG Has Been Here, pp. 53–54
Yoko, pp. 14–15

Long vowel sounds
Thunder Cake, pp. 24–27

Punctuation
Frog, Where Are You?, pp. 87–88
Something BIG Has Been Here, pp. 53–54
Quotation marks:
Martha Speaks, pp. 83–85

Syllables
Something BIG Has Been Here, pp. 53–54
Zin! Zin! Zin! A Violin, pp. 50–51

Vocabulary awareness
Something BIG Has Been Here, pp. 53–54
Descriptive language:
Best Friends, pp. 17–18
Owl Moon, pp. 32–33
The Purple Coat, pp. 89–91
The Relatives Came, pp. 77–81
Plural endings:
Frederick, p. 82
Rhyming words:
17 Kings and 42 Elephants, pp. 44–47
Feathers for Lunch, p. 49
Noisy Nora, pp. 48–49
Social Studies:
Where the Sidewalk Ends, p. 54
Synonyms:
Dr. DeSoto, p. 83
Something BIG Has Been Here, pp. 53–54
Words with −ed/−ing endings:
When I Was Young in the Mountains, p. 91
Speaking and listening skills
Chrysanthemum, pp. 15–16
Miss Malarkey Doesn't Live in Room 10, pp. 13–14

MATH
Addition
Seven Blind Mice, pp. 65–66

Counting and estimation
A Chair for My Mother, pp. 66–67

Graphs
The Bookshop Dog, pp. 67–68

Measurement
A Chair for My Mother, pp. 66–67
Time (calendar):
Frog and Toad Are Friends, pp. 71–72

Ordinal numbers
Seven Blind Mice, pp. 65–66

Patterns
Knots on a Counting Rope, pp. 61–63
Night Tree, pp. 33–34

Number Stories
Seven Blind Mice, pp. 65–66

Numbers
Emily's First 100 Days of School, pp. 8–12
How Much Is a Million?, p. 64

Size and shape
A Chair for My Mother, pp. 66–67
The Grouchy Ladybug, p. 69

SCIENCE
Conservation
Miss Rumphius, p. 73

Living things
Animals:
Stellaluna, pp. 72–73
Plants:
Tops and Bottoms, p. 70

Teaching With Favorite Read-Alouds in First Grade